T5-CCV-771

Margaret M. Self

G/L
REGAL
BOOKS

A Division of G/L Publications, Glendale, California, U.S.A.

© Copyright 1977 by G/L Publications
All rights reserved

Published by Regal Books Division, G/L Publications
Glendale, California 91209
Printed in U.S.A.

Library of Congress Catalog Card No. 76-62687
ISBN 0-8307-0517-1

*Grateful appreciation is expressed to Joanne Feldmeth
for assistance in preparing this book.*

CONTENTS

FOR THOSE WHO GUIDE YOUNG CHILDREN

"NOW what can I do?" A plea familiar to every adult who shares his life with a young child. The pages in this book contain more than one hundred answers to that question!

Christian parents, however, are interested in more than simply keeping their child pleasantly occupied. Those parents who love the Lord and value His Word realize the importance of helping their child learn spiritual truths at an early age. For parents who sometimes feel at a loss in knowing how to accomplish that task, the guidelines in this book make an excellent starting place.

HOW DO I BEGIN?

Establish now the habit of being available to your child—of regularly setting aside time to give him a bit of your undivided attention. Parents who allow themselves to be "too busy" during these formative years lose one of their most important opportunities to instill spiritual values into their child's life.

WHAT DO I TRY FIRST?

Select from this book activities that you feel you and your child will enjoy. Although all the activities are planned for young children, there are many differences between the abilities and interests of a two-year-old and a kindergartner. A two-year-old will usually be content with a slapdash approach, then announce, "I'm done!" while a kindergartner will be able to work more independently and for a longer time. Remember, for young children the process—the fun of doing—is more important than the finished product.

The activities you select will depend on your interests as

well as your child's. And for that reason we've included activities involving art, cooking, gardening, music, language development and outdoor exercise.

This book wasn't meant to be read from cover to cover but rather like a book of recipes. When you find something that appeals to you and your child, jump right in and try it. Scribble notes in the margins indicating how well your child liked the project or a variation you want to try the next time.

Most of the activities require only basic supplies or throw-away household items. No activity requires more than twenty-five minutes, some less than ten. However, all have a definite purpose to teach or reinforce a developing skill or scriptural concept.

A bit of preparation for these activities—particularly the art projects—can save you time and simplify working on them. Begin by reserving a cupboard, drawer or shelf to store discarded wrapping paper, construction paper, scissors, pencils, crayons, glue, a paste brush, masking tape, several colors of tempera paint and a paint brush. If you're keeping supplies on a shelf, organize them in shoe boxes or plastic bins. Tuck in a boy's or man's discarded shirt from which you have cut the sleeves and collar. When your child paints, button the shirt on him down the back.

WHERE DOES THE TEACHING COME IN?

With each activity are conversation ideas suggesting ways to use the project to teach spiritual truths. Use these suggestions to talk naturally to your child about a particular Bible truth. Utilizing everyday opportunities to reinforce your child's concept of God and to teach scripturally-oriented values is an art. However, it's an art you can develop quickly with a little practice, time and thought.

Children have a knack for spotting hypocrisy! To gain your child's confidence in spiritual matters requires that you be completely committed to your values. It also requires your willingness to show your love to your child by being available to talk, to listen and to spend time with him in a mutually rewarding experience.

WHAT SHALL I DO WITH THE FINISHED PRODUCTS?

Young children enjoy seeing their art work displayed and valued. So get out your masking tape and turn the refrigerator or the hallway into a family art museum. No interior decorator can match a child's art for a personal touch with very special charm! When the masterpieces come down, store the larger paintings in a suitbox or large art folder. Smaller flat pieces can go into a scrapbook and bulky crafts will fit into a cardboard box.

WHAT ABOUT THOSE TIMES WHEN I'M RUSHED?

Although the bulk of this book provides ideas for projects to do *with* your child, we know that all too often, the "NOW what can I do?" question comes at moments when a parent simply cannot spare any time—that hectic hour before dinner or a morning that must be dedicated to finishing a term paper, fixing the car or making an important phone call. It is especially for those moments when your duties and your child's boredom collide that we have included the "What to Do When Everyone Else Is Busy" section. Here is a collection of imaginative activities for your child that does not require your close supervision.

We hope this book provides starting places for strengthening your relationship with your little one; for guiding his thinking toward scriptural values; and for giving you a bit of inspiration in your challenging job of parenting.

Margaret M. Self

A Special Note to Teachers

Although this book is primarily written for parents, almost all of the activities are easily adaptable to classroom situations. When a particular idea applies to a preschool or kindergarten setting, we've labeled it with a "Classroom Clue" design.

THINGS TO DO WITH PAPER, SCISSORS AND GLUE

Glue

Note: For easy pasting, pour liquid glue in a shallow foil pan. Provide a paste brush (available in art supply or stationery stores) for child to use in spreading glue (or starch) onto paper.

FOR YOU AND YOUR CHILD

One of the priceless gifts you have within your power to give your child is the gift of allowing him to acquire feelings of security and trust. Trust, that sure feeling of belonging, is learned in infancy and nurtured carefully during these early years. Family members play key roles in providing an atmosphere in which their little one can acquire these feelings of trust.

In a secure environment, he finds courage and confidence to explore, to attempt new activities and relationships. His boldness is rooted in his belief that things will go well for him. And if they don't, he knows he can retreat to the safety of his parents.

A child's development is often a zigzag pattern, and seldom a smooth inclining plane. Yesterday he was the brave adventurer, readily trying new food and making new friends. Today he's returned to babyish ways of behaving. He seems to have lost his taste for squash; an unfamiliar face sends him hurrying to your arms. Every child needs to feel assured he can safely retreat if growing up becomes more than he can manage. This retreat must be easy, not just in physical terms, but in emotional ones also. The child needs to feel he will be accepted when he rushes back to safety, with no ridicule of his fearful hesitancy or fears. The support of family members in times of stress does not result in hampering a child's development. Rather, it provides him a reservoir of strength to face difficult moments. Family members who have the patience and confidence to let a child set his own pace give the child a priceless gift of security.

Make a Family Tree

You need...

- Snapshots of family members and relatives.
- Paper, crayons, scissors, glue.

YOU...

1. Cut snapshots to include one individual picture of each person.
2. Sketch a tree outline as shown.
3. Talk with child about each person and their relationship to him.
4. Help him know where to place each picture.

Your child...

Glues pictures to paper.

As you work, talk about the pleasant facets of each family member's personality. Help your child recall happy experiences he has had with that person. When you feel your child is receptive, say, "Let's thank God for making our family." Then pray briefly, thanking God for family members.

FOR YOU AND YOUR CHILD

For a young child, the world is filled with wonder, just waiting to be touched and examined. And God has well equipped him with the tools to satisfy his insatiable curiosity. These tools are a child's five senses—his ability to see, hear, touch, taste and smell. Now all he needs are repeated and varied opportunities to explore his world. And here is where thoughtful parents can help. The spring and summer months provide some of the best times to help your child explore the wonders of God's creation. There's no need for an exotic setting to enchant one so new to the marvels of God's world.

Simply point out a snail meandering up the sidewalk, a trail of ants in the dirt, a dandelion blossom or a caterpillar on a leaf. These evidences of God's handiwork will fascinate your little one. As a thoughtful parent, you'll want to do more than just expose your child to the out-of-doors. Share with him your feelings of joy and excitement for the things God has made. Your own consciousness of God as Creator helps to inspire your child's feelings of wonder. In this spirit of shared enjoyment, explain briefly a few simple facts about the object that has caught the interest of your child. For example, "See the veins on this leaf. Feel them with your finger. What color is the leaf? God made leaves. Thank you, God, for green trees with leaves." "What a beautiful web the spider has made! The web is sticky so it will catch flies for the spider to eat. Just look how the web shines in the sunlight."

"Guess the Picture" Game

This simple guessing game in which a child sees only a portion of a picture at a time helps him focus his attention on picture details he might otherwise miss.

You need...

- Several colorful pictures of things God has made, such as plants and animals.
- One piece of paper for each picture; a manila envelope the size of the paper; glue.

You...

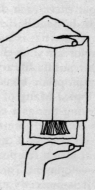

1. Trim and glue pictures on pieces of paper.
2. Place pictures in envelope.
3. Pull a few inches of one picture (at a time) from envelope; let child guess what he thinks picture might be. Continue gradually revealing more of the picture until he has guessed correctly.

Your child...

Attempts to guess the object in the picture from small section you show him.

As you enjoy this activity together, help your little one know, "God made these lovely red roses. Our Bible says, *God made every thing.* I'm glad, aren't you!"

FOR YOU AND YOUR CHILD

One of the most heartening signs parents see in their child's development is his instinctive attempt to break away from the total dependency of infancy. He's growing up! And now as never before, he needs your guidance in knowing how to handle the new and exciting experiences each day offers. Begin by familiarizing yourself with what is normal behavior for your child's age. (Your public library has appropriate books on this topic.) Many of the most trying things a child does are not only normal characteristics of a certain age, but also a temporary stage of development. For example, it is perfectly natural for a child to be curious about the contents of kitchen cupboards. (If he showed no interest in the world about him, something would be seriously amiss.) When it is necessary to restrict his behavior, avoid labeling the behavior as naughty or bad. Substitute an acceptable activity for the forbidden one. It is very frustrating to a child to be told what he CANNOT do, without being told what he CAN do. Each day thank God for the alert mind and energetic body He has given your little one. Also, ask the Lord for His help in guiding the development of this precious life God has loaned to your love and care. "If you want to know what God wants you to do, ask him, and he will gladly tell you, for he is always ready to give a bountiful supply of wisdom to all who ask him; he will not resent it. But when you ask him, be sure that you really expect him to tell you, for a doubtful mind will be as unsettled as a wave of the sea . . . If you don't ask with faith, don't expect the Lord to give you any solid answer" (James 1:5-8, The Living Bible).

Young children need many opportunities to learn about their world and the things in it. They need to handle and use a variety of materials. Collage making is an ideal activity to provide that kind of firsthand experience.

You need...

- Paste or glue
- Scrap materials for pasting, such as fabric, colored paper, dry cereal (no flakes), macaroni, feathers, leaves, seashells, buttons, rickrack, etc.
- Heavy paper or lightweight cardboard.

YOU...

1. Demonstrate each technique listed for your child to do.
2. Talk with child about materials he is using, and the physical skills he has developed. Express thanks to God for your child's ''hands to paste these leaves.''

Your child...

1. Selects item to paste onto cardboard.
2. Applies paste to paper.
3. Presses item onto paste-covered area.
4. Repeats process with as many items as he desires to use, placing them in any design that appeals to him.
5. Helps clean up and puts things away for use another time.

FOR YOU AND YOUR CHILD

There is nothing like a puppet to change a shy child into a chatterbox. Words and imagination seem to flow naturally from any child who picks up a puppet. After your child has completed his puppet (see opposite page), ask the puppet questions and let your child answer. Or suggest he and you act out his favorite story.

Puppets are an excellent way to include your little one in your family times—those moments when family members think and talk together about God's Word and how it relates to everyday experiences. For example, family members may use the animal puppets to put on a short skit about sharing or being kind. Be sure puppets talk about a way to resolve their problem in terms of obeying God's Word. A family may want to make several paper bag puppets of Bible characters or purchase "More Paper Bag Puppets" from a Christian bookstore. Use the puppets to act out simple Bible stories. Your youngster will enjoy being a part of these activities.

CLASSROOM CLUE In addition to using puppets to tell a story, consider them for giving directions. When children need to be quiet, or to sit or stand, let a puppet make the request. Use a puppet to make announcements, introduce a visitor or a new class member. Children also enjoy having a puppet say, "Wiggle your nose." "Hold up four fingers," etc.

Paper Bag Puppets

You need...

- Lunch-size paper bag for each puppet.
- Construction paper in assorted colors.
- A piece of orange fringe (available at yardage stores).
- Glue, crayons or felt-tip pens and scissors.

You...

1. Enlarge patterns.
2. Cut animal features (ears and elephant trunk) from appropriate colors of construction paper.

Your child...

1. Glues the animal features to the paper bags as shown in sketches.
2. Uses felt-tip pens or crayons to add eyes, whiskers, mouth, etc.

Elephant's trunk Elephant's ear Rabbit's ear Dog's ear Cat's ear

FOR YOU AND YOUR CHILD

The Lord Jesus came to restore people to physical, mental and spiritual wholeness. After He had touched them, these people felt a newness of life. As a parent you have the exciting task of working in cooperation with God's timetable to guide all areas of your child's developing personality. An essential ingredient in this growth process is your child's realistic sense of self-esteem and independence. He needs to feel the satisfaction of doing some things (although they may seem of little consequence to adults) for himself. Unfortunately, children live in a world designed for adult skills. Their attempts to use adult-oriented equipment often result in mishaps and failures. You can help to off-set the impact of these frustrations for your child by observing a few simple procedures: **Buy your child clothing which is easy for him to manage, thus enabling him to take care of a significant share of dressing and undressing himself. Show him which is the front of a garment. **Provide low, open shelves for your child's playthings, so the toys are seeable, reachable and returnable. Shallow plastic notion containers offer good storage for put-together toys. **Install low hooks and easy-to-open drawers so your child can help to get out and put away his clothing. Include a clothes hamper so he can place his dirty clothing in the right place. **Allow ample time at meals so your child can feed himself without your taking over to feed him. As your child attempts to do things for himself, praise him for his efforts. Even a failure can be satisfying when you recognize his intentions.

Make a "Helping Book"

Increase your child's awareness of the people who help him by directing his attention to specific incidents. For instance, when the postman delivers the mail, say, "I'm glad our postman brings us our mail. He is a fine helper." Also, include reference to the librarian when you visit the library; your child's church school teacher, the nurse in your doctor's office, etc. Also include family members.

Suggest making a "Helping Book" by selecting magazine pictures to represent each helper. Trim the pictures. Let your child paste one picture per page in a scrapbook or a greeting card catalogue (remove the cards). Beneath each picture, letter the kind of help the pictured person gives.

On the last page place a picture of the Lord Jesus. Beneath it letter, "Jesus loves us. And we love Jesus."

FOR YOU AND YOUR CHILD

When two children reach for the same toy at the same time, conflict usually results. And the adult on the scene must decide immediately how to resolve the problem. When you are in this situation, resist the temptation to deliver a lecture on the virtues of sharing. A child who is emotionally upset is not likely to understand or be interested in your words. Also, he would probably feel that if sharing means losing out, then he wants no part of it. The best approach with young children is to distract one child with a duplicate toy or another activity. A young child lives in a world of "I, me and mine." He has not yet progressed in his emotional development to the point where he can share something he wants for himself. Before sharing can become a part of the child's behavior pattern, he needs to experience many occasions in which someone shares with him. Also, he should have repeated opportunities to share under enjoyable circumstances. Of course, a child can be forced to give up an object to another child. However, his behavior is really obedience to adult authority rather than one of true sharing. To give your child a pleasant experience involving sharing, consider the tissue lamination activity described on the opposite page. Take turns dipping your brush in the starch and adding pieces of tissue. "First, it's my turn to dip my brush in the starch. Then it's your turn to dip your brush in the starch. I like to take turns with you. Isn't taking turns fun!" Also, in your natural conversation help your little one know, "The Bible says, 'Be very glad.' And I'm very glad we can take turns together."

Tissue lamination

You need...

- Scraps of brightly colored tissue paper.
- A shallow pan of liquid starch.
- Two brushes with ½-inch bristles.
- Lightweight cardboard or heavy paper.

You...

1. Demonstrate each technique listed for your child to do.
2. Make a tissue lamination picture, too.
3. Talk about taking turns as a happy way to work.

Your child...

1. Brushes liquid starch over cardboard.
2. Places pieces of tissue paper (in any way he chooses) on starch-covered area.
3. Continues adding alternating layers of starch and tissue paper to create interesting colors, patterns and textures.
4. Helps clean up and put things away for later use.

Note: To prevent picture from curling, after it dries, place it under several heavy books.

FOR YOU AND YOUR CHILD

Many parents who love their little one dearly and provide adequately for his physical needs have never really learned to enjoy him. Even the simplest activity adds fun to parent-child relationships: playing ball together; talking together over a cup of warm cocoa; cutting out paper dolls—or making an entire paper zoo. (See opposite page.) A parent who spends twenty minutes on a simple activity with his youngster isn't wasting his time—he is investing it.

On the day you decide to make the paper animals, assemble the necessary materials. Then sit down on the floor or at a low table so your face is at your child's eye level. As you begin making the animals, let him do as much as he can. Some kindergartners will enjoy cutting. (Do not expect adult-perfect work. Also, avoid the temptation to "take over" the project.) Keep your work-pace unhurried so your little one won't feel rushed. More than one or two rapid-fire directions confuse and frustrate a child. Use the paper animals to play zoo—making animal sounds and moving the animals. Also, play out the story of Noah and the ark after you have read it to your child from a children's Bible storybook. (See Resources, page 140.)

CLASSROOM CLUE Guide children in talking about the kind of food and home appropriate for each animal puppet.

Paper Stand-up Animals

You need...

• Construction paper, scissors. • Pencil and crayons, glue. • Yarn (for mane and tail) and buttons. • A shoe box and lid.

You...

1. Cut construction paper into dimensions in sketch.
2. Fold paper in half. Draw head and body outlines on the pieces of paper. Cut an arch from loose edge of paper to form legs and body. Use the circle pattern to cut heads.
3. To cut giraffe, see sketch. At the bottom of the neck, cut one inch into the fold so neck "straddles" the body.
4. Cut shoe box ark as shown in sketch.

Your child...

1. Glues animal's head to one corner of body (one circle on each side of fold).
2. Adds ears, tails and other features.
3. Colors the animals with crayons.
4. Uses the animals to play out Noah and the ark Bible story; visiting the zoo; an animal parade.

FOR YOU AND YOUR CHILD

Have you ever seen a two-year-old so frustrated and angry he trembled? Or, an unhappy four-year-old desperately trying not to cry?

It is easy to forget that children feel emotion as intensely as do adults. We sometimes think the Bible teaches that Christians must never have negative feelings. Not true! The Bible teaches us to recognize our feelings and deal with them in a constructive manner.

Use the paper plate mask activity (opposite page) as a way to talk naturally about feelings with your youngster. Ask, "What are some things that make you happy? (sad)?"

Be prepared for some honest responses. And be willing to accept his negative feelings. Help your little one channel those feelings into positive actions. For example, if five-year-old Sean tells you that his baby sister makes him angry because she "grabs my truck and I don't like her anymore and I want to throw her away!" it's no time to moralize, "You mustn't feel that way." Rather, acknowledge Sean's feelings. "I can see how it would make you feel angry when Beth grabs your truck. How do you think we can keep this from happening?" Work out a compromise. Perhaps Sean's special treasures can go on a higher shelf and he can play with other toys when Beth is nearby. Sean has just had a valuable lesson. He can feel angry, talk about this feeling and also resolve the problem without physical retaliation or "throwing away" his sister.

Paper Plate Masks

You need...

- A large paper plate and ice cream stick for each mask.
- Scissors.
- Crayons or felt-tip markers.
- Optional: pieces of paper, yarn, paper cup, cellophane tape or glue.

YOU...

1. Have your child hold the paper plate in front of his face. Carefully mark where the eye holes should be.
2. Cut out holes for eyes.
3. Talk with your child about how his mask will look: frightened, angry, happy, sad. He may want to make several masks, each with a different expression.
4. Make yourself a mask. Ask your child what kind of expression he'd like your mask to have.

Your child...

1. Uses crayons to draw a face.
2. Holds his paper plate mask in front of his face.
3. Optional: a paper cup can be attached with cellophane tape for a nose. Fringed or curled paper strips or strands of yarn may be glued on for hair.
4. Makes up a simple story to play out with you using the masks.

FOR YOU AND YOUR CHILD

Ever catch yourself shouting, "You're behaving like a child!" only to realize that your son or daughter is only a child, after all? We often expect too much from our children primarily because we want to look like an effective parent! Our pride leads us into setting standards that are unrealistic—standards that simply are not appropriate for our child. You may be outgoing—but your son may be shy. You may be artistic —but your daughter may be athletic. Hoping that our children will fulfill our dreams is a very selfish attitude—and it leaves little room for God's plan that each person (young or old) be a unique and worthwhile individual.

God accepts us as we are and loves us regardless of our limitations. (See Romans 5:8.) We need to help our child understand that we love him because of who he is, not because of what he can or cannot do. That kind of love provides him with confidence and self-esteem.

As you and your child enjoy the paper art activity (see opposite page) remember that his work will be much affected by his age and his interests. Avoid "constructive criticism" such as: "That's nice Tom, but make the loops more even." Tom's not fooled—he knows you don't really think "it's nice." Rather, compliment him sincerely on the colors or shapes he's chosen or simply tell him you're glad he's having a good time.

Paper Strip Flowers

You need...

- Colored construction paper.
- Paste.
- Crayons.
- Scissors.

You...

1. Cut the construction paper into strips and other shapes.
2. Demonstrate making two flowers: one with strips and one with loops while your child watches.

Your child...

1. Creates his own flower designs.

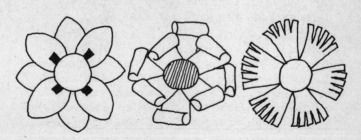

More things to do with paper, ✂ and glue

1. Patchwork pictures: Cut trees, people, houses, etc., from different colors of construction paper or fabric. Paste them on a sheet of white paper.
2. Self-portrait: Have your child lie down on a long piece of shelf paper. Trace his outline. Then he pastes on buttons for nose and eyes and yarn for hair; he uses paint or crayons to complete clothing details. Help him cut out the figure and mount it on a prominent place for all to enjoy.
3. Puzzle: Have your child glue a picture to a piece of cardboard. When glue is dry, cut picture into puzzle shapes. Let your child assemble pieces to complete the picture puzzle. Store in a shallow box or envelope for later use.

CLASSROOM CLUE
   At Open House display children's life-size figures about the room, building with blocks, working at home living area, looking at books, etc.

THINGS TO DO WITH PAINT

FOR YOU AND YOUR CHILD

"Donna help!" Donna announces proudly as she empties the sugar bowl into her father's cup of coffee. The "helpful" deeds of a young child grow from his natural desire to imitate the actions of the adults in his life. Although his motive may be worthwhile, his timing seems inevitably to coincide with those moments when his parents are in a frantic rush. Parents need to recognize that this powerful drive to achieve success and earn recognition is a normal part of a child's growth. God Himself has set in motion these laws of a child's developmental process. Without the desire to "do it myself," a child would forever remain dependent on others. Plan an opportunity each day that will allow your child to learn the way to perform a helpful task, no matter how small. The normal routine of daily living includes many things (raking leaves, dusting, bringing in the newspaper, putting away pots and pans or canned goods on lower shelves) he can do with minimal help when given enough time and specific direction. Often parents confuse a child by offering very general directions. Avoid, "Put your toys away." Rather, state specifically and briefly what you expect. "Put that red truck on this shelf." Be sure he completes one task before you give him another direction. Also, have many words of praise and encouragement for his efforts. Special activities also will help your child develop important skills and attitudes. The sponge painting suggestion (see next page) will improve a child's coordination, creativity and ability to follow instructions— all important to achieving feelings of success and independence.

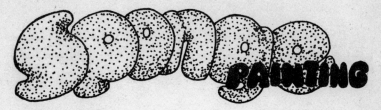

SPONGE PAINTING

You need...

- 12x18-inch pieces of shelf paper.
- Tempera paint—one color.
- A shallow pan.
- A piece of sponge 2 inches square snapped into a springtype clothespin. (Sponge is easier to cut when wet.)
- A boy's old shirt (with sleeves cut off) to wear backward as a smock.

You...

1. Pour paint into shallow pan.
2. Demonstrate the techniques your child will use; explain what you are doing at the same time.
3. Talk with your child about what he is doing; have words of praise for his efforts rather than pointing out his mistakes. "What interesting work! I like the way you paint."

Your child...

1. Dips sponge into paint, then drags it against side of pan so it will not drip.
2. Experiments in making designs by pressing, pulling, dabbing, sliding sponge on paper.
3. Helps clean up and put things away.

"Jimmy looks just like his dad!" Comparing a child to his parents is a favorite pastime of friends and relatives. Similarities in appearance are often so striking that we cannot help commenting on them. However, parents often overlook another way in which their child displays a family likeness—in his attitudes and behavior. A child's strong tendency to pattern his feelings and actions after his parents can be an exciting way to help that child learn important values. For example, to help a child learn to be concerned about other people, consider these ways of modeling the kind of behavior you want your child to adopt. 1) Speak kindly about other people. Avoid critical and negative comments. Things you say and the way you say them have a strong impact on your child's attitude toward others. 2) Be warm and friendly toward people you meet. Your child will take his cue from you. 3) Let your child see you doing helpful things for other people. Find ways to include him, appropriate to his interest and ability. Then praise him for his efforts. "Jerry, when we take dinner to Mrs. Davis, you can help by carrying the rolls. You'll be a helper, just like our Bible says to be!" 4) Verbally label your behavior for your child. "Mrs. Davis is sick today. I'm glad we can cook dinner for her." "I like to help you put on your new shoes. I'm glad I can help you." This kind of guidance builds a child's awareness of the practical applications of helping others, as well as increasing his positive feelings about helping.

Finger Painting

Here is a simple, fun-to-do activity you and your child can enjoy together. When he can do something you're doing, then he can use you as a model for his own behavior.

• For finger painting: Select one of the following: Ready made fingerpaint; liquid starch colored with powdered tempera paint or food coloring; soap flakes and enough water (about 2 parts soap to one part water) to whip until mixture is stiff.

• Good surfaces for finger painting include: any washable table or countertop; glazed butcher or shelf paper taped to table; large piece of cardboard; linoleum scraps or piece of floor tile.

As you and your child enjoy finger painting, have words of encouragement and praise for his efforts. "I like the way you make those big red circles! I'm glad God made your eyes so you can see red colors."

Be sure to include your child in the clean-up process. "What a good job you're doing wiping the table! You are a fine helper, just like our Bible tells us to be."

FOR YOU AND YOUR CHILD

"God knew what He was doing when He planned for a child to have two parents. It takes two people to carry all the stuff!" This comment from a harried young father portrays a parent as a glorified porter. During a child's early years, parenting does include many menial tasks. However, parents must not limit their vision simply to the chores involving a child's physical needs. There is another dimension to parenting that transcends all the nitty-gritty functions an adult does for a child. As a parent, you create a climate for your child that cannot be described in terms of the furnishings in your child's room, style and cut of his clothing, vitamin content of his diet or quantity and quality of the toys you provide him. Your child's emotional and spiritual growth are largely the result of the strength and love in your character and personality. Your child needs the security of a stable family to guide him, protect him and nurture him. That does not mean parents must be perfect to be effective. God never intended for angels to raise human children. God gave the task to human parents—people who make mistakes. Your child needs to live with parents who can accept and admit failures in themselves. The next time you are wrong in dealing with your child, admit your error and ask forgiveness of your child and of God. Your attitude and actions will provide a positive example for your child and will renew your awareness of God's grace as shown by Jesus' death for man's sin. Your recognition of the price God paid to atone for human failings allows you to provide the honest, compassionate guidance your child needs.

Finger Painting Outdoors

A shady spot out-of-doors, a flat surface (a picnic or folding table well protected with newspaper), the materials listed here and your understanding and enthusiastic guidance will provide your youngster with a delightful creative experience.

You need...

- Paper with glazed surface.
- Liquid starch.
- Soap flakes.
- Powdered or liquid tempera paint.
- 50¢ piece and pencil.
- Teaspoon.

You...

1. Demonstrate procedures for child.
2. Assist as needed.

Your child...

1. Outlines coin with pencil as you hold coin in place.
2. Pours starch to fill circle outline.
3. Sprinkles teaspoon of soap flakes on starch.
4. Adds teaspoon of tempera paint to starch.
5. Spreads mixture with fingers, palms, knuckles or fists.
6. When finished, washes hands, and puts away materials.

FOR YOU AND YOUR CHILD

"Oh, look, Daddy! Look at all those flowers!" Jane shouted. "Let's take a closer look," Daddy said as he and Jane walked up the hill in the park. This father realized he needed to capitalize on his daughter's interest and enthusiasm right then and there! Although he wasn't a flower expert, he helped Jane see the way the petals curled. It was easy for him to relate "God made..." to what Jane was experiencing.

Using a child's current interest and answering questions WHEN he asks are golden opportunities to teach effectively. Sometimes in our eagerness, we tell a child more than he's able to absorb. Keep your explanations within his understanding and interest. "Jeff, how does the grass feel on your bare feet? Does it tickle? God made the grass. [God] 'made every thing... God is good.'" If Jeff seems receptive, thank God for the grass in a brief moment of informal prayer.

Saturate your teaching with love. After all, the way your little one reacts to what you say depends upon your attitude. You are the child's most important teacher—not of facts especially, but of values. Your daily way of living shows your child what you really believe and what you feel is important. Your little one's world can be an exciting world of discovery. You can make that discovery so much richer when you help him know God "made every thing"— because He loves us!

Rock Paperweights

You need...

- Various-sized rocks collected on your walk (see opposite page).
- Warm, soapy water.
- Spray sealer.
- Tempera paint and brush.
- Pebbles.
- Glue.

You and your child...

1. Select a variety of rocks to decorate.
2. Scrub rocks thoroughly.
3. Decorate rocks by painting with tempera paint and/or gluing on pebbles.

When paint and/or glue is dry, spray the rocks with sealer.

Classroom clue...

Before painting rocks, guide children in sorting rocks by color, size, texture (smooth, rough) and shape (flat, round). Or, on a large piece of paper write numerals from one to eight. Child places one rock on the numeral one, two rocks on the numeral two, etc.

FOR YOU AND YOUR CHILD

A child without guidance often feels unloved and frightened because he never knows what is allowed and what is not. One of the best ways to show love for your child is to set realistic limits for him. He needs the security of knowing you care enough about him to insure his safety. During these early years, he must feel he can trust you completely for all of his needs, emotional as well as physical. Sometimes the kindest thing you can say to your child is "no." The best attitude for effective discipline is "I love you too much to let you act that way," combined with a willingness to back up your words.

Your youngster won't enjoy your enforcing limits—he or she may protest loudly. But never assume that a firm no or a well-deserved spanking will cause you to lose your child's love. As long as the corrective discipline in your home is balanced by preventative discipline— sharing time (see activity on opposite page) and love with your child—the limits you set will be further evidences that you care very deeply for your child. A noted educator has said, "The hardest thing for a child to resist is the displeasure of a parent who has built a strong relationship with him." An obedience which springs from love and respect is a joy to any parent, but more than that, it teaches a child exactly the sort of responses he needs for a healthy, growing relationship with the Lord.

SQUEEZE BOTTLE Painting

You need...

- 3 plastic squeeze bottles with very small holes in the tops.
- Paper.
- 3 colors of tempera paint.
- Starch.

You...

1. Pour a different color paint in each bottle.
2. Add about 1 teaspoon of starch to each bottle. Tightly screw lids on bottles.

Your child...

1. Tips the bottle against the paper and squeezes—hard or gently—to get the effect he wants.
2. "Draws" with the squeeze bottle by moving it over the paper.

FOR YOU AND YOUR CHILD

It's Janey's best friend's birthday next Tuesday, so you hurry into the toy store, pick out something appropriate and have it wrapped. On the day of the birthday party, you hand Janey the neatly-wrapped gift just before she races up the steps. Has Janey really given anything? No, of course not. The gift is from you. Giving can be a great joy for a child and there are ways to include even young children in the process. To make a birthday card, let your child "gadget print" the outside of a piece of folded paper—and then dictate the message for you to letter on the inside. The results are more personal and charming than a commercial birthday card, for it represents a true gift of time from your child to his friend.

Creating original wrapping paper is another way for your child to make his gift special. Even very young children will enjoy "gadget painting" (see opposite page) their own paper. Let your child select the colors of paint to use for his design. Colored tissue paper also provides interesting color contrasts. Have plenty of scrap paper on which your child can experiment before he begins his final efforts. Although young children are often more intrigued by receiving than giving, having a part in a gift to a special friend is one of the best ways to begin experiencing the joys of generosity.

CLASSROOM CLUE To make waste baskets, children cover large ice cream cartons with gadget printed paper.

42

Gadget Print Wrapping Paper

Wrapping gifts will be even more enjoyable for a young child when he uses wrapping paper that he has designed himself!

You need...

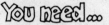

- Two shallow pans.
- Liquid starch.
- Red and green powdered tempera.
- Shelf paper.
- An assortment of "gadgets," such as corks, sponges, cookie cutters, lids, corrugated cardboard tightly rolled and fastened with rubber band, potato or carrot with design cut on one end, etc.

You...

1. Mix in shallow pans powdered paint with liquid starch so that the mixture is a thicker consistency than for finger painting.
2. Demonstrate for your child the use of each gadget.

Your child...

1. Dips gadget into paint.
2. Presses gadget onto shelf paper to make a variety of designs.
3. Helps clean up and put things away for later use.

More things to do with paint

1. Blow painting: Place a few drops of paint in center of paper. Give your child a drinking straw and let him gently blow the paint in different directions on the paper.
2. Fold-over blot painting: Fold a piece of paper in half. Open the paper. Let your child splatter paint spots on the paper; fold the paper again and press with his hand. Then open the pages and admire his picture!

THINGS TO DO WITH

EVERYDAY MATERIALS

SALT · OIL · Flour

The Bible talks about sharing as an outward response to an inner feeling. No merit is due the person who gives "grudgingly or under compulsion" (see 2 Cor. 9:7). Yet, parents often attempt to teach their child to share without really considering the child's feelings. When Jon lets Susan ride his tricycle, Mother says he has "shared" even if he screamed or pouted through the whole affair. At times it may be necessary to insist that Susan have a turn on the trike. But under no circumstances should Jon's reluctant behavior be called sharing. Neither should he be shamed for his "selfish" conduct. He is simply showing normal behavior for a child who has not yet learned an important lesson, a lesson which touches him at the core of his inner being. True sharing is most likely to be a child's genuine response when he feels happy and secure about himself. Applying pressure to surrender a treasure, even temporarily, actually makes the child less able to share since it increases his feelings of anxiousness and insecurity. Help your child build a positive self-concept by consistently accepting him and his feelings. He needs to know you love him just the way he is, especially when his behavior is upsetting and requires intervention from you. "Jon, I know you are mad. You want the ball very much, don't you? But I cannot let you hit Susan." Assuring your child that you understand his feelings and providing the security of firm, reasonable limits is a first step in helping him be ready to consider the rights and concerns of others.

Sharing Is Fun!

To give your child opportunities in learning to relate to other children of his own age, invite another child to visit in your home. (One child at a time is enough. Relating positively to more than one child at a time is often difficult and frustrating for a little one.)

Plan one activity which encourages (but does not demand) interaction. For example, on a shady porch, let children mix two separate recipes of salt/flour dough. Color one batch red, the other yellow. As each child works with his dough, it won't be long before they decide on sharing dough. They'll enjoy a pleasant surprise when they discover mixing red and yellow produces a new color!

Salt/Flour Dough

⅓ cup (.08 l) salt   1 teaspoon (5 ml) salad oil
½ cup (.24 l) flour   vegetable coloring
enough water to make a bread dough consistency,
⅓ to ½ cup (.08 to .24 l)
4–6 drops of oil of cloves or wintergreen

Mix salt, flour and water to consistency of heavy dough. Add oil, mixing thoroughly. Add coloring. Store in airtight plastic bag or jar.

Provide small-sized rolling pins and tongue depressors for children to use as they work with dough.

FOR YOU AND YOUR CHILD

The last time you were down on the floor playing with your child, did you happen to look at the room and its furnishings to see them from your child's eye-level? To him the furniture is massive, windows are unreachable and doors seem monstrous. Most of the interesting, decorative things are far from his eye-level and out of his reach. Since so much of his home is "off limits" to your child, make sure he has a sufficient number of things (in places other than his room) that he can safely use and enjoy. For example, when a young child turns through a magazine, his lack of small muscle control often results in torn pages. Select a discarded magazine to place with your magazines. With a felt-tipped pen, letter his name boldly on the cover. When he reaches for a magazine, show him his magazine. "This is your magazine. Your name is right here! This says, 'Jon'." Look through the magazine with him to help him discover pictures of animals, people and familiar foods. Kitchen cabinets seem to have an unusual appeal for a young child. Do some rearranging of your kitchen supplies so one lower section can be "Jon's cabinet." In it place a variety of discarded pots and lids, a sieve, etc. Include a percolator so your child can have the experience of assembling the parts. When clean-up time comes, include your little one in the process. Give one simple, specific direction at a time. "Jon, put these pans in your cabinet now." Have words of encouragement for your fine helper's efforts. Also, help him know, "When we put away our things, 'we are helpers,' just as our Bible tells us to be."

Make a Bird Feeder

Let your child help you make a bird feeder. The satisfaction he will derive from helping plus the enjoyment your family will gain from watching the birds are well worth your efforts to get the project underway.

Guide your child in rolling a pine cone in lard or shortening. Then let him sprinkle birdseed over the cone. Tuck in small pieces of suet, also. For a hanger, thread a piece of cord through the cone. Then select a low branch or eave from which to hang the feeder. Be sure the hanger is easily visible from your window. A weekly sprinkling of seed will insure that birds will return to it again and again.

As birds visit the feeder, ask your child simple questions to help him discover interesting features. "What color is that bird's head? How do the birds keep from falling off the branch?" Also, help your child know, "You were kind to help the birds have food. You are a kind helper!"

FOR YOU AND YOUR CHILD

"Let me see the kitten!" says Marsha although she has an unobstructed view of it. What Marsha really means is "Let me touch the kitten." Like all young children, Marsha wants (and needs) to be close enough to an object not only to see but also to feel it. Adequate exploration of his world requires a young child to use more than one of his senses. We often ignore this important aspect of a young child's development for our years of experience enable us to recall a wide range of impressions from a simple stimulus. For example, when we hear a sound, we can call to mind what the object making the sound looked like, how it felt, smelled or tasted. Not so for a young child!

He hasn't yet lived long enough to possess this backlog of associations. He needs repeated and varied experiences with his environment so that he may accumulate a similar kind of backlog. God has wonderfully equipped each child with the ability to see, hear, touch, taste and smell. Increase your child's learning by helping him use several of his senses. For instance, provide brief and simple experiences pertaining to your routine activities. As you operate your vacuum cleaner, suggest he place his hand on the cleaner to feel the motor vibrate; also let him feel the suction. Show him where the dirt accumulates. Consider the ideas on the opposite page to expand your child's learning by offering him a variety of opportunities to explore his world. And have fun!

Learning Experiences

• Place several familiar food items on the table in front of your child. Let him name each one. Cover his eyes (do not insist if he seems fearful). Then offer him each item, one at a time. Let him guess what he is eating. Ask questions about how it tastes and how it feels in his mouth. "Is it salty? Is it hard?"

• Place a cotton ball in each of several identical containers (such as pill bottles). Saturate each cotton ball with a different scent. Include perfume, vinegar, food extracts, such as orange, lemon, mint, maple flavorings. Ask child to smell and then name each scent. You'll probably need to supply him with words the first few times he enjoys this activity.

• Cut circles approximately 8 inches (20 cms.) in diameter from a variety of textured fabrics, such as velvet, net, leather, wool, burlap, felt, fur, corduroy. Also include sandpaper. Cut two circles from each kind of material. Suggest your child find matching circles.

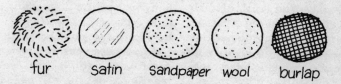

fur   satin   sandpaper   wool   burlap

• Vary the matching experience by collecting a variety of objects, such as shells, stones, leaves, buttons, spoons. Your child will enjoy separating them into like kinds.

As your child works at these tasks, help him know in your natural conversation, "God made your eyes to see which circles are alike. *God cares about you!*"

FOR YOU AND YOUR CHILD

An important part of a young child's learning has to do with his ability to name the objects he sees and uses every day. Few things are more familiar to him than the parts of his own body. Yet parents often neglect to help their child to know and name body parts accurately. Begin by showing your little one his reflection in a mirror. "Touch your hair. What color is your hair? . . . Touch your eyes," etc. Then reverse the game. You touch his hair, etc. Let him tell what you are touching. Another time help your child identify his head, shoulders, knees, toes, etc. To "Mulberry Bush" tune, sing, "Head and shoulders, knees and toes . . . Let's all sit down together." Child touches body part you sing about. After he's become familiar with his head, shoulders, knees and toes, substitute the names of other parts of his body (elbows, ankle, waist, heel, etc.). When your child has mastered the ability to point to various parts of his body and name them correctly, make the game more challenging. "Ricky, put one hand on your knee. And put your other hand on your head." "Put one hand on your shoulder. Put your other hand on your elbow." An older brother or sister may enjoy this activity with him. Another time ask Ricky what part of his body he uses for a specific task. Nonsense suggestions help keep the game fun. ("Do you use your foot to brush your teeth?") Also, commenting about the part of his body he is using at the moment helps to increase his understanding. "Ricky, you are doing such a good job building with your blocks. God made your hands so you can stack those blocks just where you want them. God is good!"

Felt Faces

You need...

- Several different colors of felt.
- A piece of cardboard, 12-inches (30 cm) square.
- Scissors.

You...

1. Cut a large oval from one piece of felt.
2. Cut two eyes, a nose, a mouth, two ears, eyebrows and hair from contrasting colors of felt. See sketch.
3. Cover with flannel the square piece of cardboard.
4. Give your youngster pieces you've cut from felt and the flannelboard.
5. Talk about facial features and their purpose. Thank God for physical abilities.

Your child...

1. Arranges the felt pieces on the flannelboard to represent a face. (Expect him to also experiment in arranging the pieces in unrealistic ways.)
2. Identify the facial features as you ask, "Point to the eyes, ears," etc. Or, you point and let him supply the appropriate name for each feature.

FOR YOU AND YOUR CHILD

"Christy, I'm going to the hardware store—how about coming along and keeping Dad company?" What a boost to your child's self concept, for it's a spontaneous indication that you enjoy being with her. Sometimes the responsibilities of being a parent confuse our priorities. We get so caught up in "getting things done" that we relegate to our children only our leftover time and energy. The result is we often miss out on precious moments we could share with our little ones. Sometimes, of course, there are times when you really need to work alone. However, an occasional sacrifice of the efficiency of doing it yourself is well worth the joy you will bring to your child by including him or her in the odd moments of your life.

Sometimes that involvement can be as simple as pausing in your Saturday morning gardening to give your youngster a ride in the wheelbarrow. On other days, set aside more time to ride on the merry-go-round; pick out a new puppy; or string macaroni jewelry. (See opposite page.) A good follow-up project for the macaroni art is to make a "jewelry box" by covering a powder box with gift wrapping paper and lining it with cotton. As you and your little one enjoy moments together, verbalize the happy feelings you both are experiencing. "I really like giving you a wheelbarrow ride! I'm glad we can have fun together, aren't you? And I'm glad God planned for you to be my little boy!"

MACARONI JEWELRY

You need...

- Macaroni with large holes.
- String, yarn or shoelace.
- Tape.

You...

1. Make a "needle" by wrapping a piece of cellophane tape tightly around one end of the yarn or string.
2. Help tie on the first and last "bead."

Your child...

1. Strings the macaroni, one piece at a time.
2. Leaves some string at each end for tying.
3. Tries on his new creations: necklace, belt, headband and/or bracelet.

Variations...

1. Color the macaroni by placing it in a mixture of food coloring and water or tempera paint. Remove macaroni with tongs or a slotted spoon. Let dry on waxed paper overnight. Draw and color a pattern (see sketch) for your child to follow as he strings colored macaroni.
2. Use drinking straws (cut into 1½-inch pieces) in place of macaroni.

Red Blue Yellow Green Orange

FOR YOU AND YOUR CHILD

Learning to express his thankfulness to God is an important step in a child's spiritual development. To catch the spirit of prayer, your little one needs repeated opportunities to hear you pray. He keenly senses your attitude of reverence and sincerity. As he consistently hears your expression of thanksgiving and praise to God for His loving care, your child soon begins to recognize that God is living and cares about people, including himself. When your child is present, make your prayers brief and simple. Avoid using archaic terms, such as Thy, Thou and Thee. Talk to the Lord about things within your little one's experience. During your daily routine, you'll find many opportunities to guide your child in a brief prayer of thanks to God. Avoid using terms such as "all the things." Be specific! For example, as you walk through fall leaves, say to your child, "Just look at this pretty red leaf! God made this red leaf. Let's thank God. 'Thank you, God, for these pretty red leaves, Amen.'" As your child helps to put away his toys, say, "I'm glad God made your strong arms so you can lift those heavy blocks. We can tell God thank you for making your arms. 'Thank you, God, for Brian's strong arms, Amen.'" A young child also needs to know the people in his family are an expression of God's love for him. Be alert for opportunities when a family member has shown kindness to your youngster. Then say, "Daddy fastened the wheel back on your truck. Aren't we glad for Daddy! God knew you'd need a daddy to help you. God made Daddy. We can say, 'Thank you, God, for Daddy.'"

PRESSED-LEAF PICTURES

You need...

- Fall leaves of different colors, sizes and shapes.
- Crayons cut into small shavings.
- Wax paper sandwich bags.*
- Newspapers.
- Yarn or string.
- Warm iron.

Your child...

1. Selects and arranges leaves and a few crayon shavings inside wax paper sandwich bag.

You...

1. Place the sandwich bag between folded sheets of newspaper. Iron newspaper surface gently several times.
3. Remove sandwich bag. Punch two holes at the top of bag. Tie with ribbon or yarn for hanger.

Your child...

1. Hangs his picture in a window for a "stained glass" effect.

*Or, use a folded sheet of wax paper.

1. Popcorn art: The next time you make popcorn (and before you butter and salt it!), save some for popcorn art. Have your youngster draw three circles (one above the other) on a piece of paper. Then he pastes the popcorn inside the circles to represent a snowman. He may add raisins for facial features.

2. Surprise picture: Place a small object (a coin, a paper clip, a cardboard geometric shape such as a circle, triangle or square, etc.) underneath a piece of paper. Show your child how to rub over the paper with the side of a crayon (from which you have removed wrapping). The crayoning will pick up the outline of the object. Next time, let him arrange several small objects under the sheet of paper in his own way.

THINGS TO DO WITH FOOD

FOR YOU AND YOUR CHILD

When you say, "Susie, let's have some juice and a cracker," Susie probably accepts your suggestion eagerly. Generally a young child finds eating a delightful experience. This ready-made interest in food serves as an ideal opportunity to help your little one learn about food sources. For example, milk is a familiar food to your child. So what could be more interesting than introducing him to a cow? Even for city dwellers, dairy cows are usually accessible with a little looking. Plan a family outing to a nearby dairy to provide an opportunity for your child to learn about the source of his milk. To increase your child's enjoyment and avoid the possibility of his being frightened by the size of a cow, prepare him for the event. Begin talking about this outing several days ahead. Show him pictures of cows. Talk about what they eat and how the milk is obtained. Practice imitating the sounds cows make: let your little one chime in. At the dairy lift your child up in your arms so he is not overwhelmed by the animal's size. Approach the cow slowly, as you talk about things you have discussed. Point out the physical features of the cow; also explain the milking process in simple terms. Plan your trip so your child can see the cows being milked. In your natural conversation, comment, "I'm glad God made cows. Aren't we glad for their good milk to drink!" After the dairy visit, remind your child of the things he saw. As you pour his milk, say "Where did this milk come from? . . . And God made those cows!" Pray, "Thank you, God, for helping Susie have this good milk to drink, Amen."

Let's Make Instant Pudding

As a follow-up to your dairy visit (see opposite page), let your child help you make instant pudding. He can pour the package contents into a deep bowl, add a premeasured amount of milk, and take turns with you in stirring the mixture. Encourage him as he works. Praise him for his efforts. Talk about the things he does correctly, rather than pointing out his mistakes. Before eating the pudding, pray, "Thank you, God, for making cows to give milk. Thank you for Eric's strong arms that helped stir the pudding, Amen."

FOR YOU AND YOUR CHILD

Summer is an ideal time for your child to learn about foods in their natural state. Also, examining and tasting fresh fruits and vegetables provide an opportunity for you to help him discover that God is the source of all food. A backyard garden or a window box planted with small vegetables allows a child to observe the stages of growth. However, his observation will probably be superficial unless you share in the activity. "Brian, let's look for some little green leaves. Do you see any? Good for you! Let's count them." Examinations of progress should be kept brief. Help Brian know, "God sends warm sunshine to help our plants grow. Thank you, God, for the sunshine." A drive in the country can provide a pleasant family outing as well as an enriching opportunity to let your child see a variety of food crops. Visit fields growing fruits or vegetables familiar to your child. Stop the car and get out to let him have a close-up inspection. (Saying, "That's corn growing," as you whiz past a cornfield is not conducive to a young child's learning!) His interest and his learning take a giant step when he is able to find out for himself what is growing. The moment of discovery is an excellent time to thank God for that particular food. Follow this outing with a visit to a bookstore or library to find picture books of growing plants. The book you choose will give you another opportunity to help your child know "God sends the warm sunshine and cool rain so (tomatoes) can grow. Mm! Tomatoes taste good! I'm glad God helps us have tomatoes to eat. God cares about us."

Meet Brian, the Cook

Plan simple food preparation experiences in which your youngster can have a part. Of course, working alongside his favorite adult (you!) is an important part of the fun. Let him help you . . .

Shell peas Sustain his interest by suggesting, "Let's count the peas in your pod. I wonder how many are in your pod."

Scrub baking potatoes Give him a scrubbing brush (with a handle he can manage) and a bowl of water.

Make butter Pour a pint of whipping cream at *near room temperature* into a jar. You and your child take turns shaking until butter separates. Pour off liquid. Pour ice water over butter and drain. Sprinkle lightly with salt. Serve butter on baked potatoes.

FOR YOU AND YOUR CHILD

Perhaps the most worthwhile and effective guidance any parent can give his child is to help that child build positive and loving feelings toward the Lord Jesus. To begin, consider these suggestions. First, remember that the way a child feels about a situation is usually the basis for his actions. For example, his interest in stories about the Lord Jesus will generally be a reflection of the way you feel about those stories. When you consistently read and talk with him about Bible stories, he begins to sense they are important to you. And he gradually accepts this attitude as his own. Second, within the atmosphere of an accepting and loving home life, a child begins to build feelings of trust—that sure sense of safety and belonging. These satisfying relationships with the adults in his life serve as a foundation for building a loving attitude toward the Lord Jesus.

A child needs to consistently hear (within the context of everyday routine) you make references to the Lord Jesus in your natural conversation. For example, when you (or someone you know) have a specific need, explain it briefly to your little one. Then say, "We need to ask the Lord Jesus to help us." At the time your family experiences a pleasant surprise, comment, "Aren't we glad for the way Jesus loves and cares for us!" When you feel need for the Lord's forgiveness, say, "I want to tell Jesus I'm sorry I spoke angrily to Janet." As your child senses your dependence on the Lord Jesus in all aspects of your daily living, then your little one, too, will begin to think of Jesus as the One who loves and cares for him.

Make Biscuits

From a child's Bible storybook read about Jesus cooking breakfast for His friends (John 21:1-13). Then suggest, "Jesus cooked good food for His friends. Let's cook something good for our family to eat." Hot biscuits for breakfast (or dinner) will be a welcome surprise.

You need...

- Biscuit mix and ingredients called for in the recipe on the box.
- Unbreakable mixing bowl, large spoon, biscuit cutter, baking sheet.

You...
1. Arrange equipment so child can work easily and safely.
2. Demonstrate each step; explain briefly what you are doing.
3. Give assistance only when necessary.
4. Handle all steps involving oven.

Your child...

1. Pours premeasured ingredients in bowl, then mixes ingredients.
2. Pats dough on floured board; cuts out biscuits with cutter.
3. Helps clean up while biscuits bake.

FOR YOU AND YOUR CHILD

Jeff seemed very pleased that his cousin Lynn had arrived for a visit. But when Lynn began to play with Jeff's toys, he grabbed his treasures and screamed, "Mine! Mine!" Although Jeff's reaction was typical for a two- or three-year-old child, nevertheless, some of the unhappiness could have been lessened by preparing Jeff before Lynn's visit. Parents need to include a child in getting ready for a visitor, whether the visit is only for a morning or a longer stay. If the house needs cleaning or food prepared, help the child feel part of the activity. As you work, explain briefly to the child what you're doing and why. Labeling your actions with words is vital to increasing a child's understanding. "Marsha and her mother are coming to eat lunch with us.

You can help make lemonade for all of us to drink." (See opposite page.) This involvement with your preparation helps your child see you getting ready to share your things with others. Modeling the kind of behavior you want your child to exhibit is an essential part of his learning. Next, let your child select the toys that he wants to make available when the visiting child arrives. Any toys not to be shared should be put out of sight until the visitor has left. As you and your child make preparations, have words of praise and encouragement for his efforts, no matter how trivial they might seem to you. "Jeff, Marsha and her mother will like this lemonade you're helping to make. You know how to 'do good things,' as our Bible says to do."

Make Lemonade for a Friend

Here is a recipe your child can help you **read**

tablespoons

Sugar

tablespoons

I CUP

FOR YOU AND YOUR CHILD

Have you ever attempted to determine what was happening in a room by looking through a keyhole? Then you have some idea of your child's restricted view of his world and the people in it. The things he does observe often move too rapidly and are too complex for him to evaluate and absorb adequately. So, he must depend on watching your reactions to know how he should respond. Long before your little one could understand the meaning of your words, he could sense your emotional temperature. For example, when he sees you willingly and graciously showing thoughtfulness and kindness to other people, he senses those actions are good and that this is the course of action he should follow. When he sees you being friendly with his church school teacher, and hears his family speaking positively about people at church, then he will be more likely to trust and love the people with whom he comes in contact at church. It's helpful to your child if he observes your demonstration of hospitality within the familiar surroundings of his own home. Occasionally invite your child's church school teacher to your home for lunch or a backyard picnic. Also, invite your pastor and his family to share a freezer of ice cream or some other summertime treat with your family. Remember that negative comments and criticisms also have their effect on your child's emerging attitude toward people and places. Again, he takes his cue from you. If your child does not see and feel your examples of loving kindness, all the talk you can muster will do little to convince him he should be loving and kind.

No-Bake Cookies

Let your child help make cookies to enjoy and to share with others. This recipe requires minimum adult help, thus giving your little one the satisfaction of doing most of the work himself. Guide your child in mixing together (in a deep bowl):

½ cup (.12 l.) raisins
½ cup (.12 l.) finely chopped dates
2 tablespoons (30 ml.) honey

Then let him use a rolling pin to crush several graham crackers in a plastic bag. Make sure the air is out of the bag before rolling begins. Let him mix enough crushed graham crackers with the other ingredients so mixture is dry enough to roll into balls.

Then suggest he taste the efforts of his labor. Help him deliver cookies to family members or friends.

As you work together, talk about the happy events of the Christmas season. "We are glad for Christmas because Christmas is Jesus' birthday."

More things to do with food

1. Apricot Coconut Balls: In a large, deep bowl, guide your child in combining 1½ cups or a 6-ounce package (168 g) of *ground* dried apricots and 2 cups (.47 l) of flaked coconut. Stir in ⅔ cup (.16 l) of sweetened condensed milk. Show your child how to shape the mixture into small balls. Let him roll the balls in confectioner's sugar. Store the balls at room temperature until firm.
2. Fruit Shake: Let your child put 1 cup (.24 l) cranberry juice, ¼ cup (.06 l) orange juice and 1 cup (.24 l) vanilla ice cream into your blender container. Cover and process at "stir" until smooth. This mixture makes about 2½ cups (.59 l) of refreshing "fruit shake."
3. Stuffed Celery: Cut celery stalks in 2-inch (5 cm) lengths. Let your child stuff each piece with peanut butter.

THINGS TO DO WITH PLANTS

Helping a child learn to say thank you at the appropriate moment usually ranks as a high priority task in parents' thinking and planning. However, most parents realize simply training their child to say the right words without helping that child grow in his feelings of gratitude results in a hollow and meaningless experience. An important way for parents to help children develop feelings of thankfulness is to consistently demonstrate expressions of thanksgiving themselves. A child needs to observe parents responding in a variety of situations with heartfelt gratitude. Unfortunately, many children hear parents express almost nothing but negative feelings. How easy to let our complaints overpower our compliments! This week plan to consciously share with your child your thankfulness to God. For example, while you're helping your youngster get dressed, say, "I'm so glad God gave me such a fine boy! I thank God for you, Jeff." When you are out-of-doors, "Aren't these yellow leaves pretty! God made the leaves so many colors. Thank you, God, for making these pretty leaves for us to enjoy, Amen." These honest expressions of your feelings expressed at the appropriate moment, help your child to sense your response to God for His goodness to you. To help your little one enjoy the excitement of discovering God's plan for growing things, consider the "Plant a Seed" suggestion on the opposite page. As your little one watches the daily progress of a plant he helped to start, guide him in expressing to God his praise and thanks for this evidence of God's love.

Plant a Seed

You need...

- Seeds, such as lima beans
- Water
- Cotton
- Flower pot
- Potting soil

You...

1. Soak seeds overnight.
2. Demonstrate each action your child will take.
3. Verbally label your child's actions. Praise his efforts.
4. Periodically help your child look for signs of growth. As it seems natural, pray briefly, thanking God for making the plant to grow.

Your child...

1. Places seeds on cotton.
2. Pours water into cotton. Keeps cotton moist until seeds sprout.
3. Digs hole in soil; places seed in hole and covers it.
4. Adds water to soil as needed.

FOR YOU AND YOUR CHILD

Your child is growing right before your eyes! Have you noticed he is more than one-half his adult height? He has lost his baby fat. His muscles are becoming stronger and his coordination is improving. Growing is a topic of keen interest to each little one! Few things are more intriguing to a child than the idea of "being big." A child's emotional and spiritual development, although not as apparent as his physical growth, is nevertheless as real. Just as you provide a balanced diet, regular sleep patterns and adequate clothing, also consider the assistance your child requires for his emotional and spiritual growth. For example, to help him be aware of ways God loves and cares for him, consider this idea. When you notice a new skill or interest your youngster has developed, make a point to add this thought to your exclamation of enthusiasm. "God made your strong legs so you can climb those steps all by yourself! God loves you, Terry." "Susan, you stacked all your blocks so nicely! I'm glad God made your eyes so you can see to stack your blocks." These spontaneous moments are an especially effective time for a parent to communicate simple yet vital scriptural truths. A child needs to know how God's love and care relates to him in terms of his own experiences. What better way for a child to truly sense God's love than in those cuddly times when Mom or Dad says, "I love you very much...and God loves you, too." This feeling of being loved by his parents and by God provides a child with a solid foundation for developing a sense of trust, first in the adults about him and then in God.

Grow a Sweet Potato Vine

Watching a plant's leaf and root growth day by day is an excellent way to increase your child's awareness of God's plan for growing things.

You need...

• Toothpicks.
• A sweet potato.
• A jar.
• Water.

You...

1. Stick three toothpicks into the wide end of a sweet potato.

Your child...

1. Places the potato in the top of a jar.
2. Adds water until about half the potato is covered.

Keep the potato in a dark corner for about two weeks to hasten sprouting. Then place it in a sunny window. Add water as necessary.

As you and your child watch the vine grow, help him to be aware of God's plan. "God made the water (sunshine) our vine needs to help it grow. And God helps you to grow, too. What has God made to help you grow strong and tall?" . . . (food, sunshine, nighttime for sleeping, fresh air, etc.).

FOR YOU AND YOUR CHILD

As you observe your child's actions from time to time, are you often startled to see and hear a younger version of yourself? Hopefully, these incidents are also the occasion for some serious thought about the tremendous impact your example has on your child's behavior. For example, have you asked yourself, "How can my actions help my little one learn to show concern and helpfulness toward others?" Perhaps no better way exists than for your child to observe your thoughtful and considerate behavior toward others, and especially toward him. A young child will have difficulty learning to consider the feelings of others until he has experienced firsthand the unconditional love and acceptance of his family. As you go about helping your child in his everyday routine, identify your actions with words. Also, help him know helping each other is a way to obey God's Word. "Joey, I'm glad I can help you put on your socks. I'm glad you can help by holding very still. We 'help each other' just as our Bible tells us to do." Another essential ingredient in your expressions of helpfulness is your obvious enjoyment in the activity. A child needs to sense that doing things for others is a source of pleasure, rather than discomfort. For instance, as you prepare a treat to take to a shut-in, say, "Won't Mrs. Davis be happy for this good-tasting soup! I can hardly wait to see her smile when we bring it to her." When your examples of helping are done lovingly instead of grudgingly, your child will likely develop a positive attitude toward doing things for other people.

It's Time for Bulb Planting

Springtime provides an excellent opportunity to help your child deepen his appreciation and understanding for God's gift of lovely flowers. Secure some crocus (hyacinth, narcissus, jonquil) bulbs from a nursery. Carefully read instructions on the package; gather the materials suggested for planting the bulbs.

Show your child the bulbs and the pictured flowers on package label. "Only God can make the dry brown bulbs grow into lovely yellow flowers, like these flowers in this picture!"

Let your child arrange the pebbles and bulbs in a bowl and then add water.

As he works say, "How do the stones feel? the bulbs? Which ones feel smooth? Close your eyes. Can you tell which one is a stone and which is a bulb when I put them in your hand?"

Periodically check on the bulbs in the following weeks to add water and to note their growth. Ask your child, "How are our bulbs different today?" When bulbs bloom, pray, "Thank you, God, for these lovely flowers."

"Let's go for a walk!" your child suggests. What's your usual response? "I can't go right now...we'll go later ..." or, "Run and play... Mommie's busy"? When you actually go, do you really help him explore the world around him? How long has it been since YOU noticed the beauty of a butterfly or the flight of a bird? Discover again the wonders in God's creation, then share your awareness with your child. When he learns to use his ears and eyes under your guidance, he finds that, indeed, "the earth is full of the goodness of the Lord." Once your child catches the feeling of wonder in watching a ladybug crawl over a leaf or in looking up at the stars on a clear evening, it will be hard to keep up with his enthusiasm! Be patient while he stops, looks and listens. Young children need time to absorb new experiences. A child's interest often helps us sandpaper our dulled senses so we can thrill again to the fragrance of a rose, or be amazed at the intricacies of a spider's web. Again and again you'll say in your natural conversation, "Randy, just feel this (soft, green grass) God has made for us...God 'made every thing...God is good!' I 'thank God' for the (grass)." As you guide your child to see, hear, smell, touch and taste God's wonders, you are bringing him to a realization that God is the Creator and Giver of all good gifts.

Start a Terrarium

You need...

- Fine gravel.
- Potting mix.
- Small houseplants.
- A glass container such as an aquarium, fish bowl, large jar or widemouthed juice pitcher.

You and your child...

Put a 1-inch layer of fine gravel in the container. Add 3–4 inches of potting mix. Plant the small houseplants in the potting mix. Add small rocks, bark or moss for decoration. Add water. Cover the terrarium with a tight fitting removable cover or plastic wrap. When moisture forms inside the terrarium, remove the cover until droplets disappear. Replace lid. When soil feels dry, add a small amount of water.

More things to do with plants

1. Reserve a section of your flower bed or garden for an easy-to-grow crop, such as radishes or lettuce which your child can help to care for and harvest. Let him make a rock border for his garden.
2. Fill an empty spray bottle with water and let your youngster refresh your houseplants with a mini-shower. You may want to first move the plants out of doors.
3. Cut several carrots so about one inch of each carrot remains attached to tops. Place them in a shallow dish. Put a few stones around carrots to hold them erect. Add water. You'll see some growth after the first week.
4. Sprinkle bird or grass seed liberally on a wet sponge. Keep sponge damp. Place in a sunny window. Growth will appear in about 7–10 days.

THINGS TO DO WITH MUSIC and SOUND

FOR YOU AND YOUR CHILD

Each of us can hear when we are born, but we must LEARN to listen. Your child's ability to listen attentively is a significant factor in his academic achievement as well as his overall development. Often a child's seeming reluctance to obey results not from deliberate disobedience, but from his not listening to what he was told to do.

Young children are notoriously casual listeners! To help your child acquire listening skills, consider these ideas. If you expect him to listen attentively to you, then he needs you to provide an example by listening attentively to him. Of course, you can't stop what you're doing each time he speaks to you! But do stop and give him your focused attention now and then so he will know what attentive listening is like.

During your daily routine, call your child's attention to unusual sounds, such as a bird's song, an airplane's roar or the rhythmic chatter of a jack hammer. Play the listening game suggested on the opposite page. Also have your child stand with his back to you and count the number of times you strike a spoon against a pan. Consistently read to your child. Include Bible stories from a children's Bible storybook. Frequent your public and church library so your child can make his own book selections from books appropriate to his age level.

The World of Sound

You need...

- A tape recorder.

You...

Record a tape of familiar
household sounds.
Include a:
doorbell ringing
clock ticking
hair dryer
dog barking
washing machine
vacuum cleaner
car horn
voices of family members.

Your child...

Listens to the tape and identifies the sounds.

NOTE: If you don't have a tape recorder, have your child close his eyes and identify the sounds you make (ring a bell, hold a watch to his ear, etc.).

To help your child know God gave him the gift of hearing comment, "Aren't we glad God made your ears so you can hear that jet plane!"

Classroom clue...

This idea adapts well to classroom use. Also, tape record a class activity without telling the children. Have the class listen to the tape and identify what they hear.

FOR YOU AND YOUR CHILD

To a young child few things in his world are more fascinating than animals. Although he is not yet ready to take over the welfare of a household pet, experiences with animals are an essential part of his learning. Regular visits to a children's zoo where your child can touch the exhibits give him a valuable firsthand experience with animals. Of course, if you live on a farm, you have your own animal collections with which your little one can make friends. You and your child can also observe many kinds of animals at a park. Birds and squirrels are usually quite obvious. And what better place to get acquainted with a wide variety of dogs!

If dogs are allowed to run unleashed, be sure to be close at hand to avoid an incident that might dampen your child's enthusiasm for animals. Pet shops are also good places to see animals, even when you are only window shopping. Each encounter with an animal opens the door for you to help your child know God made all things. However, references to God as the maker of everything in our world is too general to have real meaning for a young child. He needs specific examples! For instance, say in your natural conversation, "God made this beautiful squirrel. God made everything. God is good." Ask simple questions to help your little one see an animal's unique features. (Unless an adult guides his observation, a child has often "seen" an animal in a few seconds.) Also, compare the animal to him by saying, "Do you see the squirrel's ears? God made his ears. God made your ears, too. Touch your ears. How many feet did God make for the squirrel? How many feet did God make for you? Touch your feet. . . ." etc.

"Animal Sounds" Game

These suggestions will help acquaint your child with the sound animals make and will also provide a pleasant experience you and he can enjoy together.

• Name an animal. Your child imitates the animal's sound. Then reverse the game. Your child names the animal while you make the sound.

• The next time you and your youngster go to the park or out into the woods, sit down in a quiet spot. Listen carefully to identify the sounds you hear.

• As you look at a picture book of animals, imitate the sounds of each animal you see in the picture. Your child points to the appropriate animal. Looking at a book of animal pictures is an exceptionally good follow-up experience to visiting a zoo or farm.

• Secure a record of bird and/or animal sounds. Listen to the record with your child to help him identify each sound.

FOR YOU AND YOUR CHILD

Have you discovered the joy of singing with your little one? Music is a delightful way to communicate with young children! Also, a song often expresses a child's feelings of love and praise more naturally than words alone. "But I'm not musical," you may say. Your musical skill is really unimportant. However, your interest and enthusiasm are essential!

The songs to which a child is most responsive relate to his world of family, home and friends. Be alert to everyday situations in which God's love is clearly expressed to your child. For example, when Daddy mends a favorite toy or your family enjoys an outing together, help your youngster be aware that God has planned for his family to love and care for him. "God is good to give us our family! God really cares about you, John. Let's sing about that." To the familiar "London Bridge" tune, sing,

"I am glad that God loves John, God loves John,
God loves John. I am glad that God loves John,
And God loves me, too."
Also sing,
"I am glad that John loves God,
John loves God, John loves God,
I am glad that John loves God,
And I love God, too."
To "The Farmer in the Dell" tune, sing,
"O, Jane has new red shoes,
Yes, Jane has new red shoes,
God helps us have the things we need
And Jane has new red shoes."

STATUES GAME

You need...

- A record player, a radio or musical instrument.

You...

1. Explain "While the music is playing, you can move around. But when the music stops, you 'freeze' and do not move. You hold your position just like a statue!"
2. Provide music (turn on the radio, record player or play an instrument—anything from a piano to a kitchen pan and spoon).
3. Occasionally stop the music; pause for a slow count to five, then begin the music again.

Your child...

1. Marches, skips, twirls or hops to the music.
2. Holds as still as he can when the music stops.

Children seem to have an endless variety of ways in which they express their happiness. Perhaps one of the most delightful is singing. As you've listened to your little one at play, you've probably heard him repeat bits of a familiar tune in a sing-song manner. Perhaps you've been amazed to hear him perform (with surprising accuracy) the jingle of a television commercial. How quickly a child absorbs what he hears! Use your youngster's interest in music to increase his awareness of the world about him. As you sing to your little one about everyday happenings, include specific details, such as the color, name or number involved. For instance, to "Farmer in the Dell" tune, sing, "Here is Tom's red shirt. Here is Tom's red shirt. We'll snap the snappers, one, two, three, Tom has on his red shirt." Also, singing simple directions to him is a delightful change of pace. To "Old MacDonald" tune, sing, "Tom, please put away your blocks. Stack them on this shelf." Make sure that songs about the Lord Jesus are a part of the music your child hears regularly. There is no need to make a conscious effort to teach these songs. Simply sing them as you go about your daily routine. He will quickly catch the words and soon chime in with bits of the tune. He likes to hear the same few songs again and again. He doesn't tire of repetition, as do grownups. To "Twinkle, Twinkle Little Star," sing, "Jesus is my best friend. Jesus is my best friend." Select additional songs from "Little Ones Sing" songbook (see page 141).

God Made Me!

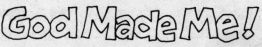

I have hands that will clap, clap, clap!

I have hands that will clap, clap, clap!

I have hands that will clap, clap, clap!

God has made my hands.

* Additional stanzas:

2. I have feet that tip, tiptoe.
3. I have fingers that snap, snap, snap.
4. I have fingers that move like this.
5. I have knees that will bend like this.
6. I have hands that will be so still.
7. I have hands that will lock up tight.
8. I have arms that will reach up high.
9. I have lips that will (whistle).

Words: Margaret M. Self. Music: Jeanne P. Lawler
© Copyright 1962 by G/L Publications.

FOR YOU AND YOUR CHILD

In a single morning you and your youngster can create instruments for an entire band! All the materials needed are those you have around the house. For instance, the roll from paper towels makes a fine horn. Or, cover one end of the roll and poke holes into it for a flute. Tape closed the lid of an empty oatmeal box or coffee can, add a spoon and you have a drum set. Slip a comb into a folded piece of waxed paper; put your lips over the fold and hum a song, moving the comb back and forth. You've made a kazoo! Use two pan lids for cymbals. For bells, hang metal kitchen accessories—vegetable grater, spoon, fork—from a circle of string. Hold the string with one hand while you strike the accessories with a spoon in your other hand. Follow the directions on the opposite page to make a tambourine. Distribute the instruments to your child and his friends and let them march around the room accompanied by music from a record or radio.

Encourage your child's interest in music by giving him opportunities to hear professional musicians. Find out if special concerts for children are held in your area. Attend an outdoor concert in the park as a family. Your kindergartner may enjoy sitting in on a portion of your church's special music programs or singing in a children's choir. As you and your child enjoy a musical experience say, "Wasn't that a pretty song! I'm glad God made our ears to hear music, aren't you!"

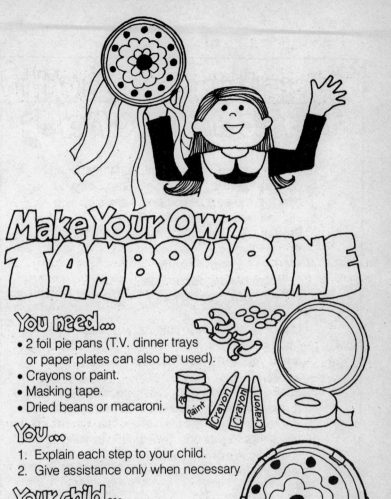

Make Your Own TAMBOURINE

You need...

- 2 foil pie pans (T.V. dinner trays or paper plates can also be used).
- Crayons or paint.
- Masking tape.
- Dried beans or macaroni.

You...

1. Explain each step to your child.
2. Give assistance only when necessary

Your child...

1. Decorates the pie pans with crayons or paint.
2. Places dried beans or macaroni on one plate.
3. Lays the other plate face down over the first plate and securely tapes the edges together.

More things to do with music and Sound♪

1. Keeping time: Choose a simple, familiar song such as "Twinkle, Twinkle Little Star." Clap your hands to the beat as you sing. Now, stop singing and clap out the beat.

2. Rhythm talk: Chant the following two lines in a singsong voice:
   "Everybody *clap* hands,
       clap hands, *clap* hands.
   Everybody *clap* hands...
       just like this!"
   Clap your hands each time you say "clap." Use "stomp feet," "pat knees," "wig-gle," "flap arms," etc. with actions appropriate to the words.

3. Poetry: An excellent way to introduce your child to the rhythm of language is to read simple rhymes and poems to him. Also, talk with him about rhyming sounds. Take turns in thinking of one-syllable rhymes, such as cat-hat-sat. Don't insist that all his rhymes be words.

4. Activity Music: Play *More Sing-Along Songs for Little Ones* record (see page 140) to encourage a child's participation or for his moments of quiet listening.

5. Share with your little one the finger fun poems from *202 Things to Do* and *Creative Finger Fun* (Bible Stories). See page 140.

THINGS TO DO WITH Words and Imagination

FOR YOU AND YOUR CHILD

Your child's first words were probably the names of familiar people, objects and activities. He began his vocabulary with these kinds of words because the adults in his life used them repeatedly as they put the words into action. "Shoe," "doggie," "go to bed" and "eat" became meaningful as he heard the words in connection with a specific action and/or object. The growth of your child's ability to understand others and express himself is largely dependent on what he hears you say and sees you do. He also needs to hear you identify with words the actions and objects that catch his attention and interest. Listening attentively when your child talks to you encourages his language development. Ask simple questions to help him clarify his thinking. Take time to answer his "What's that?" questions in a prompt and patient manner. Also, use the "Happy Talk" ideas on the opposite page. Your child's understanding of Bible truths basically grows in the same manner. He can begin to identify God as the source of all good things as he hears you consistently thank God for specific blessings. (Pray briefly using words your child can understand.) He comes to think of God as the One who cares for him when he cuddles in your lap and hears you say, "Terry, I love you and God loves you, too." Recognize your child's use of a new word with the same enthusiasm you show when he acquires a new skill. Help him to associate God's love and care with this new triumph. "Mario, I'm so glad you know how to ask for a drink. God helps you learn how to say those words. God cares about you!"

Happy Talk

You may not be aware of it, but every day you play a happy little game with your child—you talk with him. Your attentiveness makes this game lots of fun for him. And it allows you the opportunity to increase his awareness of new words and concepts.

• The color game—During your daily routine, call your child's attention to a specific color. "I like your blue shirt. My pants are blue. The sky is blue. Can you point to something else that is blue?" Remember that a child's color recognition comes slowly. But his awareness of colors needs to begin during these early years.

• The shape game—"The wheels on your tricycle are round. Do you see something else that has wheels? . . ."

• The face game—"Where is Trudy's nose? Where is Daddy's nose?" Include ears, eyes, arms, elbows, etc.

• The name game—"Who is my favorite little girl?" Follow this question with a list of girls' names. Each name will probably elicit a vocal "No!" until you say the right one!

• The food game—Young children seldom notice what other people are eating. If your child is a reluctant eater, suggest, "Daddy eats a bite of peas. Heather eats a bite of peas."

Remember, a game should be fun for both you and your child. When it stops being fun, it's time to quit.

FOR YOU AND YOUR CHILD

How long did it take your child to discover which of his actions gained your approval? Not very long! A young child is highly motivated to please the adults in his life. He desperately needs that adult approval to establish a sense of his own value and self worth. When you say, "I liked the way you came when I called. You were really listening," your child receives deep feelings of satisfaction. Also, he knows specifically what he did that won your praise. And he's likely to repeat that behavior. However, if you say, "You are such a good boy," the child has no way of knowing exactly which of his actions merited your approval. So he's at a loss to know the kind of behavior to repeat. For your words of praise to be most effective, they should focus on a specific action, thus increasing the likelihood of repetition. Also, the praise must be realistic. A set of scribbles need not be pronounced as "beautiful," when the child was simply playing with crayons. A simple statement describing what the child did is sufficient. ("I like the pretty red colors you used in your drawing.") Otherwise, praise becomes hollow and meaningless as the child gradually learns that what he did was not as spectacular as the words had indicated. Honest praise, directed at the child's behavior, not his person, helps him feel good about himself and what he can do. Parents who reinforce their child's desirable behavior are demonstrating their love for the child in a way he can understand.

Are You Listening?

When your child shows you his newest treasure, what do you say?

"That's nice, Billy."

"Very good."

"Um-hmmm."

How can you continue to appear interested in the twenty-seventh scribble or the nineteenth leaf he displays for your inspection and approval? One of the best ways is to serve as a commentator, describing briefly the features of each item:

"This leaf feels soft."

"You used red and blue crayons."

"I like to smell these flowers."

An effective approach is to mirror what you think are your child's feelings:

"You really like ladybugs!"

"I like to hear you laugh while you paint. Painting makes you happy."

As your child's ability to use words improves, encourage him to comment, then reflect his comments. For example, when your youngster shows you a picture, say, "Tell me about it." If he says, "I did lots of colors," respond by saying, "You really did use lots of colors. Let's name the colors." Restating his words requires you to listen attentively. As you show genuine interest in his activities, he feels that you really do love him.

A good vocabulary is an important factor in a child's reading readiness. To increase your child's vocabulary, consider this idea. Make picture cards (see opposite page for directions) and use them for these vocabulary-expanding games:

MATCHING CARDS: Child matches pictures of like objects; or sorts them by general subject (people, food, animals, etc.).

RIDDLE CARDS: Make up a riddle for your child to answer by handing you the appropriate card. Ask questions such as: "Show me a picture of something that rhymes with 'hat.'" "Show me a picture of something that starts with the same sound as 'dog.'"

PICTURE STORY CARDS: Have your child place several cards on the table in a row. Begin with the first picture, then proceed to the second, etc., and tell a "story" about the pictures. For example: "The 'cowboy' got on a 'boat' and sailed to a far-off land where he bought a 'cat' that ate 'pink ice cream.'" As soon as your child catches on, he takes a turn to make up a story. Another excellent vocabulary game requires a small box with a lid and a plastic animal or a paper doll. Ask your child to put the toy "in the box," then "on the box," or over, under, in front of, or behind. Then reverse the game. He gives the directions while you move the toy.

Make sure your child understands words you use in Christian-related experiences. When a word does come up that he may not understand ("worship," "love gift," "praise," etc.) take time to explain it in terms he can understand.

VOCABULARY CARDS

You need...

- Pictures of familiar objects.
- 5x8-inch note cards (or make your own from construction paper).
- Glue.

You...

1. Cut pictures from old magazines and catalogues. Make sure your picture includes only ONE subject; avoid using a picture with several different people, animals or objects.
2. Ask your child to identify the pictures you've chosen.

Your child...

1. Pastes each picture to a separate card.
2. Uses his cards to play vocabulary games (see opposite page).

FOR YOU AND YOUR CHILD

Holding your bored or fretful child on your lap and spinning a tale—with his help—about a child who "looked a lot like you!" is guaranteed to capture his attention and interest. Why? Because he immediately identifies with the character. The child sees himself acting out the silly or serious imaginary deeds.

By casting your little one as the hero or heroine, you give him or her a special feeling of importance and self-worth. For example, as Heather hears about "Amy" who also happens to have blonde hair and green eyes and will be four years old in May, she eagerly supplies details, since she is the resident authority on this sort of little girl. Every child has a vital need to feel he belongs—that he is loved and valued by his family. As you share time with your child and communicate his importance to you, you're helping him build a positive self-image so essential to his personality development! For unless a child feels good about himself, he has difficulty in relating to others. What did the Lord Jesus say about the importance of thinking well of oneself? He used it as a criterion for our relationship to those about us. Jesus said, "Love your neighbor as yourself" (Matthew 19:19).

CLASSROOM CLUE Post children's name cards on bulletin board. Help children see likenesses and differences, e.g., shortest and longest name, similar beginning letters, etc.

Making Up Stories

On those days when your imagination has the blahs, plug into your child's storehouse of ideas! Begin the story by introducing a character that sounds suspiciously like your child: "Once there was a four-year-old boy with brand new tennis shoes. One day when the little boy was in his back yard, what do you think he saw?" Pick up your child's suggestion and weave it into the story: "Yes, he saw a big turtle! What did the little boy do?" Keep asking questions and "telling" the story as your child supplies the details.

As your child becomes more adept at story-telling, he'll enjoy making up nonsense sentences with you. Rather than stopping and asking questions, begin with open-ended sentences and let him complete the thought:

YOU: "I saw a sheep standing…"

CHILD: "…on the table."

YOU: "I saw a sheep standing on the table. She was knitting a…"

CHILD: "…sweater."

YOU: "I saw a sheep standing on the table. She was knitting a sweater. It was as long as…"

FOR YOU AND YOUR CHILD

The Bible tells of one "generation which neither knew the Lord, nor the work which He had done" (Judges 2:10, "Modern Language Bible," The Berkeley Version.) The rest of the passage recounts the sad plight of those who were ignorant of God and His plan for their lives. Helping your child know God through His Word is your parental responsibility before God. Perhaps you're wondering how the Bible, recounting the events of centuries ago, can possibly be relevant to a child of today? One of the most remarkable things about God's Word is the fact that the human needs with which it deals are timeless. To help your little one grow in his enjoyment and understanding of the Bible, consider these ideas— Make daily Bible reading a part of your own life. Few things communicate more effectively to your child than your attitudes and actions. Each day read (or tell) a Bible story from material your child brings home from Sunday School. Since repetition is a necessary ingredient in each child's learning process, tell the stories again and again. The more often he hears a story, the more he enjoys it. As you tell the Bible story, hold the booklet so your child can see the story picture. He needs to see visual illustrations to sustain his interest and to help him know the meaning of the words he hears. Begin Bible storytime by repeating "My Bible" (see opposite page). Tape a picture of the Lord Jesus inside the front cover of your Bible.

My Bible

I open my Bible,
What do I see?
A picture of Jesus,
He loves you and me.

More things to do with Words and Imagination

1. Pick-a-pair Game: Collect a pair of everyday objects such as crayons, spoons, socks, empty spools, small rocks. Place one of each object in two paper bags, one bag for you and one for your child. Remove an object (spool) from your bag and say to your child, "Find another spool." Your child reaches into his bag without looking and finds the spool. He says, "Here is the spool." Continue until all pairs are matched.

2. Opposites Game: Explain the concept of opposites to your kindergartner by giving several examples such as tall-short; up-down; mother-father. Then say one word and have your child give its opposite. After a few times, reverse the procedure by having your youngster think of a word and you can name its opposite.

3. Riddles: Help your child make up riddles about familiar foods and animals, community helpers, family members.

THINGS TO DO WITH ARMS and LEGS

FOR YOU AND YOUR CHILD

Too often we think of obedience as though it were simply a matter of our child submitting to parental strength and authority. "You do it because I say so," or "If you don't do what I say, you'll be sorry," are demands for obedience based solely on an authoritarian concept. However, a child's response to this kind of guidance is usually tinged with resentment. And his obedience is likely to cease when he is away from the person with authority. Lasting obedience has its roots in a relationship of loving trust. The child needs to feel that the authority figures in his life (his parents or substitute parents) care deeply about him. Then the child is able to accept their commands, knowing his parents only ask him to do what is beneficial to him. A warm, nurturing relationship between child and parent is the foundation which enables a child to really believe his parent's statement, "I am doing this for your own good." Obedience based on loving trust is likely to be continued when the child is out of his parent's presence. Scripture consistently couples God's authority with His love for His people. Faith and love are repeatedly presented as the motivators for right behavior. "If you love me, keep my commandments," Jesus said (John 14:15). Modern psychology has gathered exhaustive evidence to illustrate this truth in the parent-child relationship. The child who consistently exhibits acceptable behavior usually feels that he is genuinely loved by his parents. Simply telling a child, "I love you," isn't enough. He needs to be shown in ways he can understand.

Obey Games

Help your child learn obedience by playing games to give practice in following simple directions. These games can be played again and again, while riding in the car, waiting in the doctor's office, settling down before a nap, or just for fun.

Do what I do Use any simple movement or gesture. When you begin the game, accompany the action with words. "John, put your hand on your head, like I'm doing." When John solves that challenge, use either the action or the words. (With a younger child, you'll need to play the game slowly.) Have words of encouragement for your youngster's efforts.

Mother, may I? This is an old favorite of children. For the young child, omit the need to ask permission. Simply give varying instructions for how the child is to cross the room: tip-toe, hop, take giant (scissors, baby) steps, run, walk, etc.

Show me Name a part of the child's body (or an object in the room) for the child to touch. Then complicate the task by saying, "Touch your knee to your elbow." "Touch your nose to your knee."

What causes a child to be afraid? Why does a loud noise, a big dog or a dark room make a child fearful? Why is one child frightened by a Halloween mask while another thinks it's funny? One of the most common causes of a young child's fears is the reactions of the adults in his life. When an adult becomes upset, the impact on the child is significant. A calm, matter-of-fact manner is also contagious, thus giving the child a sense of security. How quickly children reflect an adult's emotions! Some situations, of course, harbor very real danger for a child. How does a parent go about making sure the child respects a truly dangerous situation? Parents can guide a young child safely through many experiences without subjecting the child to the paralysis of fear.

First, the child needs a safe environment to explore along with an alert adult to protect against peril. A firm "No," possibly accompanied by a quick slap on the hand, will help the child to identify those things he must not touch. Limit these reprimands to really dangerous actions. Immediately offer the child something he CAN do, in place of the forbidden activity. Talk calmly with your child about the possible results of the prohibited act. When an accident does happen, take advantage of the opportunity to help your child understand what happened. Without fixing blame or punishing anyone, explain simply and briefly what caused the mishap and what could have been done to avoid it. Always be sure the child feels he can depend on you for assistance and understanding.

Safety Games

Observing safety precautions is an essential part of a young child's learning. Consider these games to help increase his awareness of basic safety concepts.

Green Light/Red Light

Red   Green

front   back

From construction paper, cut out two large circles, one red and one green. Glue them back to back on the end of a yardstick. Provide your child with a rhythm instrument (bell, sticks, coffee can drum, etc.). Show the green circle to signal him to play his instrument. Then flip to the red circle as a signal for him to stop playing. (While he is learning, do not make changes too quickly.) When he has caught on to the game, let him control the colors while you play the instrument.

Stop/Go

While your child is riding in the car with you, talk about the traffic signals you are obeying. "I see a red stop sign at the corner. I am slowing down. Now what should I do? . . ." "I see a green traffic signal, what should I do? . . ." Soon your little one will be calling your attention to the signals and signs.

Crossing

Make a game of crossing the street by asking questions before you get to the curb. "What shall we do when we come to the street? . . . Which hand do you want to hold? . . . Which way will you look first? . . . What will you do if an elephant is coming? . . . A mouse? . . . A car? You can use the ears God made for you to listen for cars. You can use the eyes God made for you to look both ways before you cross."

FOR YOU AND YOUR CHILD

Charles Schulz, in his delightful little book, "Two by Fours," shows a disgruntled young boy muttering, "Just when I was getting strong enough to defend myself, they start telling me about sharing." Learning to share is essential for a young child to get along with others. Does learning to share come naturally to a young child—like learning to walk? Not necessarily. In infancy everything is done for him. His world is filled with people who respond to his cries and smiles, people who seem to exist only to serve him. He sees everything from only one perspective. His! He's completely unaware that there are points of view other than his own. Thus, he sees another child who has a toy he wants, not as a person with needs and rights, but simply as a threat to his own desires. How then, does a child move from being totally self-centered to demonstrating concern for others? Initially, he needs many firsthand sharing experiences in which the circumstances are satisfying to him. This is where you come in. Your child has received many things from you during his life. And he takes it all for granted. In your daily routine, help him know, "I'm glad I can give you a piece of my watermelon. I like to share what I have with you." Label your actions with words. Let your child see you sharing with others besides himself. Again, label your acts of kindness. Your role as model will set a healthy example for your child to imitate. Also, use sharing games (see opposite page) to help him enjoy give-and-take experiences.

Sharing Games

Sharing becomes attractive to a child when he has had many enjoyable experiences of give and take. Here are some fun suggestions:

Hide'n seek This perennial favorite works better with young children when an object, rather than a person, is hidden. Hide a favorite toy, making the location easy for the child to discover. The game is more fun with many short searches rather than one long one. This helps the child learn that giving up something for a moment does not mean losing it forever.

Taking turns The use of almost any piece of equipment can be enhanced by making a game of taking turns. Keep the turns brief so your child does not face a long wait. For example, seat child on the floor, legs apart. "Mary, here comes the ball to you." Roll the ball to Mary. "You caught it! Now it's your turn to roll it to me."

Duplicate toys When a child wants what another child has, it's no time for a lecture on rights or possession. Simply provide an attractive substitute or a duplicate toy. "Now Johnny has a toy; Lisa has a toy."

FOR YOU AND YOUR CHILD

The drumbeat of rain on the roof often carries a depressing message to mothers—children will have to play inside today! But do they? If a child is in good health, dress him to stay warm and dry. Then why not take him outside for a walk in the rain? Let your child reach out from under the umbrella to feel the splash in his palm. Let him poke his head into the drizzle, stomp his boot in a puddle and feel the squish of mud beneath his feet. Walk to places familiar to your child, places where he has often seen the sun shining. Help him think about the differences the rain brings—the leaves shine, the branches drip, the grass sparkles, and the birds—where are the birds? Help your child know the good things about a rainy day. "God sends rain so you will have water to drink. Trees and flowers and grass need water, too. Just look how clean the leaves are! The rain washes our sidewalk, too." At a moment when a child is caught in the beauties of the scene, quietly pray, "Thank you, God, for giving us this rain, Amen." The reverent yet happy and natural way you speak of God and His world will help your little one begin to feel God is real and very near. If it is not possible to go out in the rain, many of the same experiences are possible by watching the rain through a window. Then during a lull in the weather venture outside to let your child experience firsthand the freshly washed out-of-doors.

Walking in the Rain

When you take a walk with a young child, your destination is unimportant. Exploring things along the way is the purpose of your excursion.

During, or soon after a shower, numerable changes are readily visible. Increase your child's awareness by calling his attention to things he might otherwise miss, such as:

- The appearance of objects when they are wet (leaves, grass, soil, sidewalk, flowers, walls of a house, doors, etc.).
- The fragrance of freshly washed air.
- The feel of raindrops against his face and hands.
- Sounds, such as tires on wet streets, rain falling on leaves, water rushing in gutters or dripping off roofs, feet splashing in puddles.
- The appearance of earthworms, bugs and snails.
- Keep the excursion brief and fun. Go again next time it rains.

FOR YOU AND YOUR CHILD

For several weeks, four-year-old Monica had wandered around the new house getting into every forbidden corner and becoming increasingly moody and defensive. Finally, her parents realized that her real problem was boredom. Away from her friends and her play yard, Monica just didn't have enough to do. So her father attached a swing to a tree in the backyard and built a small sandbox. As Monica began spending time playing outdoors, she became increasingly relaxed and happy.

There is a direct and important relationship between a lack of exercise and an increase in tension and tempers. Playing outdoors is essential for the welfare of children. If you can't meet your little one's need for a play area in your own yard, then take him regularly to a nearby park or school yard. Make sure your child understands that those active arms and legs are gifts of God, and that God wants him to enjoy physical activity. If you're planning a birthday party for your child, remember to provide for outdoor play. Consider the suggestions for simple group games on the following pages. Two- and three-year-olds find it difficult to concentrate on group games and prefer to play in the sandbox or to roll a ball by themselves or with one friend. Fours and fives will enjoy these games. Remember, competition is not appropriate for any young child! Prizes are a good idea only if everyone in the group receives one.

Who Can Go?

You need...

- Chalk or ropes to outline a large circle, square and triangle on the grass or pavement. These geometric figures must be large enough for several children to stand inside.

You...

1. Call out instructions:
   "If you're wearing something green, go and stand in the circle." Pause for children to obey your instruction.
   "If you are wearing something brown, hop to the triangle."
   "Everyone wearing tennis shoes, skip to the square and sit down."
2. Continue with similar instructions as time and interest indicate.

The Children...

1. Move from one place to another, following the appropriate instructions. Commend children's efforts. "What good listeners you are! You really know about colors!"

Bean Bag Game

You need...

- Bean bags.
- Several cardboard cartons.
- 9x12-inch pieces of construction paper or cardboard.
- Chalk or masking tape.

You...

1. Clearly outline with felt pen numerals, letters or geometric shapes on pieces of cardboard for targets. If you are in an area with a paved surface, outline numerals, shapes and letters with chalk or masking tape.
2. Call out instructions: "Mark, toss your bean bag on the 4…" "Susan, toss your bean bag on the letter D."

The Children...

1. Toss the bean bags into the cartons or onto targets. Have words of encouragement for children's efforts.

CAT and DOG Game

Have children stand in a circle. One child is the "cat." He walks around the circle and taps a child who becomes the "dog." The "dog" chases the "cat" around the outside of the circle. He tries to tag the "cat" before the "cat" reaches the "dog's" place in the circle. If he isn't able to tag the player, the "dog" then becomes the "cat" and walks around the circle ready to choose another child to be the "dog."

More things to do with Arms and Legs

These are games for a group of children to play with a teacher, but they also can be done by just one or two children:

1. Animal Fun: The object of the game is to imitate animals. Here are a few to start with:

   Can you crawl like a snake?
   gallop like a horse?
   wiggle like a worm?
   hop like a bunny?
   waddle like a duck?

2. Obstacle Course: Gather cardboard boxes, lawn chairs, ropes, inner tubes, sawhorses, bricks and boards and set up an obstacle course in a yard or playground. Have a child help you demonstrate the way players are to get through each part of the course (wiggle through; jump over; crawl under). Then one at a time let the children go through the obstacle course. Applaud for all who succeed.

THINGS TO DO WITH SPECIAL DAYS

The Thanksgiving season reminds those who love the Lord of His overwhelming goodness to them. As an expression for their thankfulness to Him, they show genuine concern for their fellowmen.

In whatever way you show love to those about you, let your child share some part of the experience. He needs to have firsthand opportunities to know how it feels to be actively concerned for others. As your child sees you consistently showing love for those the Lord loves, he begins to accept these actions as the right thing to do.

Consider this idea. Check with your pastor for the name of a shut-in nearby who would enjoy homemade cookies and a brief visit. Suggest your child help you prepare cookies using the recipe on the opposite page. Let him arrange the cookies on a paper plate. Perhaps he'd like to use his crayons to decorate a paper napkin to cover the plate. Then off you both go to deliver the cookies! Talk about what you're doing. An important part of a child's learning is matching words and actions. "Timmy, we're taking cookies to Mrs. Miller because we love her. And God loves her too!"

Giving your child the opportunity to learn the joy of sharing and caring is an important first step in expressing God's love.

CLASSROOM CLUE Guide children in making the cookies and delivering them to another class, the principal and/or secretary in your school.

No-bake Bars

You need...

- ½ cup white corn syrup.
- ½ cup peanut butter.
- 3 cups Rice Krispies cereal.
- Mixing bowl.
- Waxed paper or buttered 8x8-inch pan.
- Spoon.

YOU...

1. Mix syrup and peanut butter together.
2. Add cereal.
3. Mix until cereal is evenly coated.

Your child...

1. Spoons mixture onto waxed paper, or
2. Pats into an 8x8-inch buttered pan and cuts mixture into squares.

FOR YOU AND YOUR CHILD

The magnitude of God's concern for us is reflected in the nature of His Gift. God did not send a simple token to show His interest in us. He actually came to earth Himself in the person of the Lord Jesus to demonstrate His love. Do your gifts to your child convey any of the quality of God's example? Are you giving your child what he really needs most—the gift of yourself? More than anything else your little one needs your love so he may feel a bit of the love that God has for him. This kind of love, so essential to a child's development is not the gushy or sentimental kind. It is, however, an active concern for a child's well-being in all areas of his development—spiritual, emotional and mental as well as physical. Help your child sense your love for him by consistently setting aside brief periods of time to either join in his play or simply observe his activity, whichever seems more desirable to him. Listen attentively to the things he has to tell you. Your child will catch your attitude and will derive strong feelings of security from knowing you care. Commend him for the things he does well rather than pointing out his mistakes. (The child who always hears criticism feels incompetent and has difficulty building a sense of personal worth. Such children feel inadequate and thus develop a fear of making mistakes.) Say, "I like the way you ride your tricycle. You can pedal so well! I'm glad you have fun riding it." This climate of love fosters your youngster's trust in you and helps establish the foundation for his trust in God.

BELL Christmas Tree Decoration

You need...

- A 3x3-inch piece of aluminum foil.
- A cup from a styrofoam or cardboard egg carton.
- Pencil.
- A 3-inch piece of red or green chenille wire.
- Red ribbon.

You and your child...

1. Lay the piece of aluminum foil (dull side up) on table.
2. Place cup, cut from styrofoam or cardboard egg carton in center. Hold securely with finger.
3. Pull foil up and tuck inside.
4. Press foil firmly against cup.
5. Turn cup over and poke a hole in top of bell with pencil.
6. Push chenille wire through hole.
7. Bend wire inside cup to prevent it from pulling out.
8. Form hanger by bending wire as shown in sketch.
9. Tie a piece of red ribbon on wire and hang bell on Christmas tree.

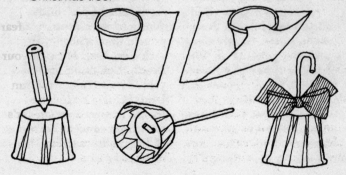

FOR YOU AND YOUR CHILD

Why does your little one seem to time his emotional upsets for the most inconvenient moment? Does he HAVE to choose your busiest day to make his presence felt? Your child is not really trying to spoil your plans. He is simply using the only approach he knows to reassure himself that you have not forgotten him in the midst of your frantic holiday activity. He does feel fearful when he senses he has become unimportant to you. Consider these suggestions to ease the situation.

• Remember your child's basic physical needs during the holidays. Sensible rest and diet patterns are vital to his well-being. • Keep a familiar book, crayons and paper, small dolls or cars at hand to interest him during an unexpectedly long wait. • Reflect to your child how you think he feels during his unhappy moments. "I know you wish we were home so you could play with your toys. You must be very tired of waiting so long here in the store." • Periodically take a few minutes from your activities to give your focused attention to your child's interests. Use "active listening"—concentrating on what he is saying rather than letting your mind race ahead to what you plan to say next. • Keep a sensible physical routine for yourself to avoid becoming overly tired. How quickly fatigued adults are irritated by a child's demands! • Continue your private time with the Lord each day. Read from His Word; then think about what you've read. Talk with the Lord. What a tragedy to let the preparations of Christmas squeeze out times of fellowship with the Christ of Christmas!

Christmas Tree Angels

Your little one will be delighted to see "a multitude of heavenly host" appear right before his eyes. He can use the paper angels as he helps you retell the story of Jesus' birth, then use them to decorate the Christmas tree.

You need ...

• Shelf paper.   • Scissors.   • Glue.

You and your child ...

1. Cut a strip of shelf paper to the width of the angel pattern.
2. Fold paper. Trace angel pattern onto paper.
3. Cut out angel figures, leaving wing points attached.
4. Decorate your Christmas tree with the angels.

FOR YOU AND YOUR CHILD

What can Easter mean to your child? Are colored eggs and chocolate rabbits the extent of a little one's involvement in the celebration of history's most significant event? What can you as a Christian parent do to help your child sense the true meaning of Easter? As in so many areas of his life, your child's feelings are largely determined by your attitude. During this Easter season, re-examine what Jesus' death and resurrection mean to you. Honest recognition and acceptance of God's great love—demonstrated at Calvary and validated by the empty tomb—makes a life-changing impact. Have you consciously and definitely responded to that love by believing in Jesus Christ and recognizing Him as Lord of your life? Your everyday, growing relationship with Jesus Christ is your most effective way to communicate the true joy of Easter to your child. Although the historical details of Jesus' death and resurrection are not yet important to your little one, he will sense and reflect your feelings of joy and praise to the risen Saviour. A child lives in the here-and-now. He can feel your happiness and wonder even though he cannot grasp the reason for it. Identify your feelings with simple words. As you and your little one go about Easter preparations, say (in your natural conversation), "Easter is a happy time. We are especially happy because Jesus loves us. And I love Jesus."

Easter Songs

Sing these happy songs of Easter to your child to help him catch the spirit of this joyful Christian festival.

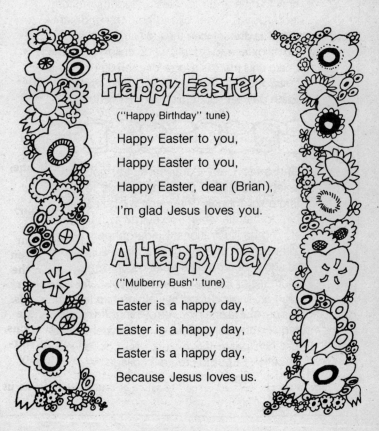

Happy Easter

("Happy Birthday" tune)

Happy Easter to you,

Happy Easter to you,

Happy Easter, dear (Brian),

I'm glad Jesus loves you.

A Happy Day

("Mulberry Bush" tune)

Easter is a happy day,

Easter is a happy day,

Easter is a happy day,

Because Jesus loves us.

More things to do on special days

1. Advent Chain: Cut 1½x8-inch strips of red and green construction paper. Show your child how to glue ends of one strip together to form loop. Use a paper clip to hold the ends until the glue dries. Insert the next strip into the first loop; glue ends. Help your child make the chain until there is a loop for each day from the first Sunday in December until Christmas Day. Each day, let your child tear off one loop.

2. Christmas Card Scrapbook: Let your child select discarded Christmas cards to paste into a scrapbook. The cards will be easier for him to handle when you cut away parts containing no illustrations. Kindergartners will be interested in arranging the biblical illustrations to show the correct sequence of events.

3. Mother's or Father's Day: Help your child design an original card by helping him find and cut out magazine pictures of things (food, clothing, hobby-related items) his parent likes. Let him paste the pictures on colored construction paper to create a collage.

THINGS TO DO WHEN EVERYONE ELSE IS BUSY

There are times in each day when it's necessary for a child to entertain himself, moments when you must attend to the needs of another child, meal preparations, a phone call. The most tempting answer is television. A few programs are suitable for young children. However, television turns a child into a passive observer when he needs experiences in which he is an active participant.

So, on the following pages are some ideas for independent play. These ideas begin by saving your cast-offs. (Children often prefer a discarded object to an expensive toy.) Your little one may spend all morning "taking pictures" with a broken camera or moving the hands on an old alarm clock. Fill a discarded suitcase with old clothes, costume jewelry, hats and badges for hours of "dress up" fun. If you have an old manual typewriter no one uses, let your child play with it; he'll have fun and at the same time get practice in letter recognition.

Armed with these suggestions and a bit of equipment, you can encourage your child's imagination—his best educational tool and his life-long antidote for boredom.

Look through the following pages for more ideas of things to save for days when your youngster needs some new keep-busy ideas. Also, jot down ideas you've thought of yourself, have found in magazines or heard about from other parents.

FOR YOU AND YOUR CHILD

"It's easier to do it myself," muttered Scott's mother as young Scott eagerly tried to find a way to help. Of course, she was right. In almost all helping situations, Scott is more of a hindrance than help. However, those bright, shiny eyes and those eager, clumsy hands are so anxious to do something for Mommy! Too often, Mommy's response to this incompetent little volunteer is to distract him into keeping out of her way. While that approach might get the dishes done sooner, it also tends to deprive a child of opportunities to learn about autonomy, achievement and self-respect. Never to contribute to the welfare of others is to miss one of life's most rewarding experiences. Why not plan a few jobs in which your child really can help? Make a list of some of the work you do. Include jobs that involve both Mother and Dad. Jot down specific things your child can do in each one. Picking up toys? Let your child find the red ones. Vacuuming the rug? He can hold the cord. Doing laundry? Let him help separate white clothes from the colored ones. Working in the yard? Let him use a child-size broom to sweep the walks and driveway. Does your family use lots of ice cubes in summer? After you fill a tray half full of water, let your child drop a strawberry, a piece of pineapple or maraschino cherry in each cube section. Later, as your family enjoys their decorative drinks, let everyone know who did the work. Your child will enjoy feelings of satisfaction and belonging— great additions to his developing self-concept.

Paint the House?!?

Or the fence, or the sidewalk, or the tricycle, or . . .

You need...
- A bucket of water.
- An old paintbrush.

You...
1. Carry the bucket to area child wants to "paint."
2. Talk with your child about his work.
3. Gather extra brushes for friends and neighbors.
4. Refill the bucket when necessary.

Your child...
1. "Paints" whatever he can reach.
2. Has fun.

Water seems to have a fascination for all young children, especially when they can experience it in manageable amounts. And what better time than summer to offer your child repeated opportunities for water play! (See opposite page.) Experiences with water also provide a variety of natural opportunities for you to help your youngster be aware of God's love and care. During your daily routine, direct your little one's attention to ways you and he use water. For example, at bath times say, "Mark, what is this in the bathtub? . . . What are we going to use the water for? . . . Did you know God made water for you? God did! 'God is good'." When your child wants a drink, say, as you fill his glass with water, "You must be thirsty. Do you like being thirsty? . . . I'm glad God made water for us to drink when we are thirsty. God loves us! Thank you, God, for this cool water to drink." As your child enjoys water play, share his enthusiasm. "Sharon, you are doing a good job 'measuring' your water. I'm glad God made water for you to use." Some parents find it difficult to use these kinds of comments. However, once a parent makes the effort, three exciting things usually happen. After the first few times a parent has included these kinds of comments into his conversation, the comments begin to sound quite natural. And at the same time, the parent becomes refreshingly aware of God's hand in the seemingly every-day things of life. And, of course, the child begins to feel that God is a vital part of daily living.

Water Play

In addition to the perennial summertime favorites, such as running in the lawn sprinkler or playing in a wading pool, consider these water-play suggestions.

Set a dishpan on a sturdy bench or chair and half fill it with warm water. Provide a variety of objects for your child to use for pouring, filling and squeezing.
• sponges
• plastic squeeze bottle
• funnel
• plastic measuring cups and bowls.
For lots of beautiful bubbles, add a
bit of liquid detergent (and a few
drops of food coloring).

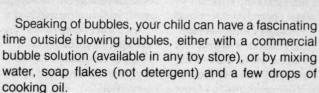

Speaking of bubbles, your child can have a fascinating time outside blowing bubbles, either with a commercial bubble solution (available in any toy store), or by mixing water, soap flakes (not detergent) and a few drops of cooking oil.

FOR YOU AND YOUR CHILD

One of the first words your youngster learned was "go," and he's been doing it ever since! A young child is usually eager to accompany anyone making a move toward the family car. Of course, you are scarcely out of the driveway before he is likely to ask, "Are we there yet, Daddy?" Short trips are an adventure for a young child. However, long treks require thoughtful preparation to insure a pleasant experience for both young and old travelers. For example, a child does not have your adult sense of time. To him, things aren't so urgent. He can't be rushed. So, plan your trip schedule to allow enough time for him to satisfy toilet needs, to nap when he's sleepy, and to eat unhurriedly. Plan stopping times to provide him opportunities to release pent-up energy and relax muscles which become tense from sitting still. Expect your child's appetite to wane. Wholesome snacks can adequately compensate for his nutritional needs. To help your little one enjoy his trip, provide Surprise Bag items. (See opposite page.) Also, sing his favorite songs with him. Read stories from a child's Bible storybook. Help him know "God cares about us wherever we go." Have words of praise for your "good traveler." Be specific! "Kenny, you have played quietly with your cars for a long time. You really know about traveling!" A well-rested, well-nourished child with a choice of activities to absorb his interest and energy will usually be a very pleasant traveling companion.

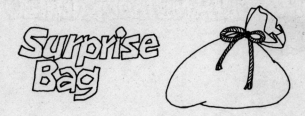

Surprise Bag

Brighten your child's travel times with a bag filled with interesting materials. Rotate his use of these items. Store in the bag those things not being used.

- 12x12-inch (30x30 cm) flannel-covered cardboard; scraps of brightly colored pieces of felt cut into outline of flowers, birds, fish, circles, squares, etc.; pieces of yarn
- picture books
- miniature doll family
- small cars, trucks, animals
- magic slate
- large red bandana or scarf
- nesting toys (lids, boxes)
- favorite doll or stuffed animal
- packets of bite-size crackers, raisins or dry cereal
- disposable towel packets
- crayons; plain paper (no coloring books!)

FOR YOU AND YOUR CHILD

Most of us remember at least one special place in our childhood—a place where we could go alone and sort out our thoughts: the corner behind the wing-backed chair, a low branch on a tree or the space under the stairway.

The feeling that one has a place of one's own is central in a child's belief that he is really important. Parents can help build their child's self-esteem by providing a place where he may keep those special treasures. A drawer or a cardboard box is fine—but it must be respected as belonging to the child. Be sure other family members also recognize, "This drawer belongs to Brian. The things in it are his. No one uses them unless Brian says it's all right!"

Once in a while, a special impromptu hiding place like the blanket house (see opposite page) is especially fun for a child. There, the world is a manageable size, and he's in charge. Add a few dolls and dishes and it's perfect for playing "house." If you have more than one child, it becomes a clubhouse. With this new place of his own, your child's imagination will keep him occupied.

CLASSROOM CLUE
Each child in your class needs his own "cubby" identified with his name. In it he places his coat, special treasures he brings to school; also items he will take home.

Blanket House

You need...

- A blanket or sheet.
- A folding table or four chairs.

You...

1. Set up the folding table or arrange the chairs so that they are in a rectangle or square arrangement.
2. Cover the table or chairs with the blanket to create a tent.

Your child...

1. Crawls in and discovers his new "house."
2. Pulls in some favorite toys and sets up "housekeeping."

Variation...

Make an outdoor version by using a discarded shower curtain or vinyl tablecloth to create a teepee.

More things to do when everyone else is busy

1. Use cardboard grocery boxes, shoe boxes and empty cereal boxes to create play stoves, trains, hiding places, tables and towers.
2. Catch a bug in a plastic bottle with holes on top.
3. Go off to an obscure corner of the backyard for a mini-picnic with some raisins, peanuts and a piece of fruit in a lunch bag. Bring along a rag doll or teddy bear for company.
4. Look through discarded catalogues and cut out "paper dolls."
5. Make a doll house from a shoe box: furnish it with a teacup bath, a pillbox bed and cut-up paper towels for linens.
6. Make a scrapbook. Use discarded magazines, Sunday School papers, snapshots, plenty of scrap paper and a lot of paste.
7. Use a paper punch to punch out hole designs in scrap paper (over the wastebasket!).
8. Arrange and paste down play stamps (holi-

day stickers, seals and stamps used to order magazines).

9. Play store—a shoebox and an egg carton make good coin sorters. Use out-dated coupons for dollar bills and buttons (IF your child will not put them in his mouth) for coins.

10. Go exploring with a magnifying glass.

11. Line up some chairs for a train or bus and go on a pretend trip. Pack your clothes in a shopping bag and use cancelled stubs for tickets.

12. Browse through a "Quiet Book"—a loose-leaf notebook filled with the activity pages brought home from Sunday School.

13. Play in the mud—a natural activity the day after a rain. Use old pie tins, empty milk cartons, wooden spoons or garden shovels and pail.

14. See how many things a horseshoe magnet will pick up (unsafe if your child still puts things in his mouth).

15. String empty spools on shoe string.

16. Sort things: the laundry, buttons, a shell collection.

17. Make a megaphone from an empty toilet paper or paper towel roll.

18. Play with a large padlock and key set.

19. Explore a semi-dark room with a flashlight; make shadows on the wall.

RESOURCES

Each of the following resources is published by G/L Publications, Glendale, CA 91209 and is available at your Christian bookstore.

- *Creative Finger Fun,* Margaret Self, Editor. 85 Bible stories in rhyme with finger fun ideas to involve young listeners.

- *Family Life Today.* A monthly magazine to encourage families in establishing and maintaining a Christian family lifestyle.

- *Little Ones Sing,* Margaret Self, Editor. Songs and activity music for young children at home, church and school.

- *More Sing-Along Song for Little Ones.* A recording of 47 selections to involve young listeners. Guitar accompaniment and conversation. Sections for listening, singing, activity, resting, marching, rhythm band.

- *The Bible Story Picture Book,* Eleanor Doan, Compiler. The Bible stories children love most written for young readers and little listeners. Colorfully illustrated.

- *You Can Have a Happier Family,* Norman Wakefield. Guidelines to assist parents in positive discipline, open communication and creative teaching, all based on biblical principles.

- *You Can't Begin Too Soon,* Wesley Haystead. Sound biblical advice and proven educational insights which offer effective ways to introduce young children to Christian concepts.

- *158 Things to Make,* Margaret Self, Editor. Creative fun and craft ideas for young children. Arranged in ten areas: God's world, prayer, family, etc., with appropriate Scripture.

- *202 Things to Do,* Margaret Self, Editor. Finger fun poems and activities to help young children understand Bible truths and experience the fun of pretending.